A COUNTRY FAMILY AT WAR

(As I remembered it)

by
HILDA BOGGIS

A Country Family at War
(As I remembered it)

ISBN No 978-0-9558844-0-5

First published in 2008
by
Rustics Publishing
15 Uplands Way
Halesworth

Printed by RPD Printers, Gorleston, Gt. Yarmouth, Norfolk

CONTENTS

Chapter 1 The Start

For weeks I had listened to my parents, their friends and neighbours quietly discussing the possibility of another war. My father who considered himself an expert on such matters and who had been gassed during the First World War when fighting over in France had said, 'The way things are shaping out, it is a foregone conclusion.'

The adults were not the only ones who discussed it. We children did too. Some of the older boys seemed excited, as if they were looking forward to it, rather than being horrified at the prospect. Their conversation now consisted mainly of Germans, Adolf Hitler, guns, ships, aeroplanes, submarines, bombs, killing and fighting. Even their games were mostly war games.

So it came as no surprise, when on the third of September 1939, at 11.15. those people lucky enough to own a wireless, switched it on and sat down to listen to the Prime Minister's speech. My family did not have that luxury as my family were poor because father could not work. Shortly after that we started back to school and our teacher quoted the Prime Minister's speech and tried to explain it.

'I am speaking to you from the cabinet room at Number Ten Downing Street. This morning the British Ambassador in Berlin handed the German Government a final note stating that unless the British Government heard from them by Eleven o'clock that they were prepared at once to withdraw their troops from Poland, a state of war would exist between us. I have to tell you now that no such undertaking has been received and consequently this country is at war with Germany. This situation in which no word given by Germany's ruler could be trusted and no country could feel safe, has become intolerable. Now we have resolved to finish it. May God bless you all. May He defend the right. It is evil things that we shall be fighting against; brute force, bad faith, injustice, oppression and persecution, and against them I am certain right will prevail.'

The whole class was silent when she had finished. Little children like us couldn't understand what it all meant, but we did take in the seriousness of the situation, though we had no idea what being at war would entail.

One of the older boys at school called me ignorant because I didn't know what a bayonet was for. He soon put me wise. 'A bayonet,' he explained 'is to jab the Germans up the backside with and make him run.' Only he didn't use those exact words.

After pondering this over in my mind, I discovered I quite liked the idea and somehow contrived to make myself a bayonet, by sharpening the end of a long stick. So eager was I to try it out, I couldn't wait for the Germans to come, so laid in wait in all sorts of likely places and made quite a few people run. Then my father, also suffering from my bayonet, grabbed it from me, snapped it in two and laid both halves across my backside. I had to carry a cushion around with me for the remainder of the week.

The first little incident of war was the thunderous sounds of gunfire out at sea. My mother explained, that enemy planes were probably firing at our ships, but I wasn't to be frightened, as it was a long way off. 'You'll have to get used to hearing things like that,' she said. 'There is a war on you know' After that we heard so much gunfire that we took no notice, other than to say if it was really bad , 'Someone is on the receiving end today.'

A few days later, when playing in the fields with my little friend Carol and her brother, we suddenly heard the most frightful sound. It seemed to rend the very air with its rising and falling notes. Terrified, I poked fingers in my ears to try and block out that dreadful sound, as did my friend. Her brother who was a year or two older stood listening in wonder. 'Gosh,' he exclaimed, a smile on his face, 'Why I do believe that is the public air-raid warning. When you hear it you are supposed to take cover.'
'What?' came my anguished moan, 'We'd better head for home quickly.
'No wait Mary,' he grabbed my arm. 'We shall have to get used to this sort of thing, there's a war on now you know.' How often was I to hear those words over the next few weeks. 'It might only be a practice, we'll hide under this bush and wait for the All Clear to go.'

6

Against my better judgement we did as he suggested and huddled together. Carol and I were shaking with fright. Her brother was shaking also, but with laughter. He wasn't a bit scared. To tell the truth I think he was enjoying it. How I wished I was brave like him.

Without warning he grabbed my arm. 'Listen' he whispered urgently. 'There's a plane coming. I think it's a Jerry. Sounds as if it's going to fly right over us.' Closer and closer it came, slowly droning along. We peered out of our bush hoping to catch a glimpse of it. There it was, high up and making a high pitched whining noise. We could tell immediately it wasn't one of our planes, it sounded so different.

'Listen to that" remarked our friend who was watching enthralled. 'Just think, there is a blooming old German airman up there inside that plane.' I watched and listened, becoming more frightened. I felt the pilot of that German plane could see us down here under this bush. Would he drop a bomb on us? How my mind ran on, but not this time. He flew straight over, then round in a circle and back over the North Sea.

Soon after came the ALL CLEAR. It sounded so different to the warning siren with its rising and falling notes. The All Clear was one continuous wail. When it ended we came out of hiding and raced home. My mother who had been anxious now looked relieved to see me. 'In future', she said , 'please remember to tell me where you are going, so if anything should happen, and pray God it doesn't, we shall know where to find you.'

One or two familiar faces had disappeared from the village. As time went by more and more gradually went, as they were called up to join the forces. One uncle had already gone and an aunt into the ATS. Later another uncle went. Grandma joined the Woman's Voluntary Services for civil defence, better known as the WVS. Grandfather joined the War Reserve Police and became a Special Constable. Mother couldn't join anything because she had my sisters Jean (the oldest), Eliza (the youngest) and me to look after.

Father felt envious. He had ran away from home to join the army during the First World War. At the age of sixteen he had added two years to his age and been over in France before his mother found out where he was. Later being the youngest in his regiment he was presented to King George V when he visited France. After that had come the gas.

After waiting in vain for his calling up papers, he plucked up courage and wrote to the war office, asking if they would accept him for a post in the army.

Then he sat back and waited eagerly for an answer. But when a letter finally arrived, it simply said they were sorry to have to turn down his application to join the armed forces. Father read it through three times before it finally sank in. He'd been so hopeful and was now so terribly disappointed. I was too, for father and I didn't usually get along very well and childlike, I had thought it a golden opportunity to get rid of him for a while.

I didn't give up however. I kept on at him. 'Father, if they say you are no good for active service, why not try for a desk job?' He looked at me with a new light in his eye.
'Yes, why not.' Eagerly he got out pen and paper and wrote off immediately, sending my elder sister down to the post box.

As the weeks slipped by, my father became more and more anxious. 'You are sure you posted that important letter of mine?' he asked my sister for about the hundredth time. 'You put it in and heard it fall down into the box?'

Nearly nine weeks had elapsed before an answer came. Father ripped open the envelope, eagerly, pulling out its single sheet of paper. Swiftly he glanced through it, then angrily slammed it down on the table and stormed outside. We waited a few minutes to make sure he wasn't coming back, then dived for the letter.

'We appreciate your determination to serve your country,' we read, 'but you cannot be accepted, not even for a desk job. Please feel comforted in the fact that you did your share during the First World War' My heart sank. So that was that, I would have to keep putting up with father.

There was a marked increase in traffic on the road these days. Mostly it was army vehicles. It was quite usual to see despatch riders on their motorbikes, tearing along the main road past the school, intent only in getting from one place to another in the shortest possible time.

We saw jeeps and big lorries too, also Bren-Gun Carriers with caterpillar tracks. The first time I saw one of those, I thought it was a tank. Occasionally, whole convoys of vehicles came along, passing us one by one. At times we wondered if it was ever going to end. The lorries were usually packed tightly with troops we would wave and cheer as they went by and they waved back at us.

Then one day my friend Charlie came to school in great excitement. 'Guess what.' He was grinning in delight at being the bearer of important news. 'A whole lot of soldiers came yesterday. They are going to camp in that wood near the house. They told my mother they are going to have a searchlight there. You know, those things that shine a big beam of light up into the sky at night, to seek out the German planes, so the guns can fire up at them.'

A searchlight so near to us. We greeted his news enthusiastically and the following Saturday a whole gang of us, led by the older boys, trooped up the road to take a look. As soon as we left the road and started along the rugged track, soldiers appeared, warning us the whole area was now out of bounds to us. We were to keep away in case we got hurt.

My mother worried, as did hundreds of others, about the blackout precautions that now had to be taken. For it was illegal to show a light anywhere at night. Drapes or blackout curtains had to be fitted to all windows. Special material could now be brought for that purpose. Mother couldn't afford to buy any, with no wage coming in, we were a very poor family.

Instead, she made a blind for the living room window, with pieces of an old blanket, then stitched lengths of brown and black material, painstakingly unpicked from two old coats, across it. It looked not unlike a patch work quilt, but when hung on hooks to the top the of the window, proved very effective. I always had a fit of giggles when she hung it up, it looked so quaint, but we soon got used to it.

Until something could be devised for the bedroom windows, we had to either undress upstairs in the dark, or undress downstairs and then go up. Not only must no light shine or show from the windows, but care had to be taken also when opening the door. Mother had an old screen that had stood in the shed for years. She now brushed the cobwebs off and brought it indoors. It was just the thing. With that and a thick blanket tacked to the top of the door. It was quite an operation every evening. First, up went the blind over the window, then the oil lamp was lit and turned down very low.

Next the screen and blanket were adjusted round the door, and mother would slip outside to take a look. One of us would then turn up the lamp, for we had no electricity. She'd then make sure not the faintest crack of light was showing.

Mother never forgot that evening when she answered a knock at the door and found a member of the Air-Raid Precautions Act, better known as the ARP, standing there.
'Madam,' he had said in a very strict voice. 'You have a crack of light showing from your window. I noticed it as I cycled along the road. If I can see it, so can the Germans if they come over. Do something about it immediately and be very careful it doesn't happen again, or I shall have to report you.'

Mother was angry, humiliated and worried. For to be reported it was said, could mean a fine; anything from three shillings to three pounds. Where would she find that sort of money? The window had been alright half an hour ago, for she had gone out and checked. Perhaps one of us children had inadvertently brushed against the blind and moved it slightly. From that day on, it was strictly forbidden to go anywhere near the window at night, without incurring my mother's wrath.

Occasionally we visited my mother's friend during the evening, to chat or just play cards. But I always dreaded the return journey, for quite often it was black dark. No lights shone anywhere. It was so easy to get lost out here in the countryside and completely lose your bearings, as we did on more than one occasion.

As soon as we were outside her friend's door, mother took hold of my younger sister's hand. My elder sister took hold of her other hand and I was on the end. While they all walked sedately homewards, I was a live wire and liked to hop, skip, or pretend I was a horse and trot. This annoyed my sister. She complained it jarred her arm. One evening her temper flared. She jerked her arm away from me impatiently. I lost my balance, fell over and rolled down into a deep ditch. All they heard was my shriek and a loud splash. Immediately my mother panicked and began shouting for help, she could hear me coughing and spluttering but couldn't see a thing.

Fortunately for me, there came a sudden swish of tyres and a weak little light came round the corner, heralding the approach of a bicycle. It just happened to be my grandfather dressed in his police uniform. He soon hauled me out, soaking wet but none the worse for my experience.

Another time we seemed lost completely. My mother had kept one foot to the to the edge of the bank, trying to decide when to turn to get us onto another road. After much foot - fiddling she said, 'Here we are. I'm sure this is the corner. We'll soon be home now.' What she forgot was, the road was only narrow and with us hand in hand spread across the road, I suddenly found myself wading in the shallow end of the pond. 'Why is it always me that comes to grief?' I wailed, as the icy water now reached up to my waist.

The reason for everywhere being blacked out was to ensure that enemy planes passing overhead could see no lights below. If they did they might be tempted to either bomb or shoot them. Perhaps they would use certain regular lights to home in on a target. The authorities got suspicious too, if a light was seen. They immediately thought you might be signalling or trying to make contact with the enemy.

We in the country were not the only ones suffering from the

darkness. It was just as bad in the towns, or so said a neighbour when we happened to mention our unfortunate experiences. They had been visiting relatives and told us there were no street lights, not that we knew anything about street lights living as we did in the country. What traffic there was, had to have their lights hooded at nights, making it awkward to see where they were going.

If you needed to have a bonfire, it was advisable to have it in the mornings if at all possible, so it had all day to burn through. As night fell it had to be doused with water, then raked apart. Apparently smoke and flames could be seen by the crews of enemy planes travelling overhead.

One day something happened that really brought the seriousness of war home to us. During the night there had been an air raid on a big town a few miles distant. At school I saw the other children huddled up together talking. 'Billy Green is dead,' they whispered.

'Billy? No! He can't be! You're mistaken,' I said indignantly, thinking they were teasing me. 'I saw him in the village shop yesterday buying his fags.'
An older boy gently touched my arm, 'that was yesterday kid. It was last night he was killed.'
I looked up into his face and could see he was speaking the truth. Nonetheless I could hardly take it in, much less believe it. It wasn't possible was it? I thought, a man couldn't be in the village shop one afternoon and dead that evening?

However it was true, as the teacher confirmed after we had said prayers. 'Children, most of you may have heard the distressing news about Mr Green and wondered why Alec, Jack and Mary are not at school today. Their father, a member of the ARP was on duty last night, working in town during the air-raid, when he was struck by a piece of shrapnel and killed. In case you don't know what shrapnel is I'll explain. When a shell is fired into the air it explodes and scatters bullets or pieces of metal. It was one of those pieces of metal that struck and killed Mr Green. A word of warning whilst we are on the subject, it is advisable never to stand outside during an air raid. It is extremely dangerous. You too could be struck by a piece of metal and killed as Mr Green was. Now we are all going to stand and be silent for one minute. During that time, you will think about poor Mrs Green and her family.'

I shut my eyes like most of my mates and thought and thought, until my mind ran riot. Yesterday they had a father and Mrs Green a husband, because I had seen him. Today they hadn't. Who would now do all the jobs at home he usually did, like digging a hole in his garden to empty the lavatory bucket in? There were no indoor toilets in these days; just a shed down the garden with a bucket inside. This last thought worried me more than anything.

However that evening something else happened that took my mind off Mr Green. My uncle came home on leave. He only had forty eight hours, but it was lovely to see him so immaculate in his smart uniform and already a stripe on his sleeve. Somehow he seemed different, older, quieter, more grown up. 'You haven't grown,' he said to me, 'not one inch since I have been away, we shall have to stand you in a bucket of manure to see if that helps.' Changed he might be, but at least he hadn't lost his sense of humour.

Chapter 2 Gas and Rations

In case the Germans decided to use gas, as they had over in France during the First World War, we were all issued with a gas mask. They were queer looking things, consisting of a large can like filter, at the front was a transparent panel to see through. To put it on you held the mask in front of your face, thrust your chin well into it, then pulled the straps held together by a buckle over your head.

We were told at school to be prepared and always take our gas masks everywhere with us. At school they hung on the backs of our chairs. They had come in a cardboard box to which a string or cord was attached. We just slung them over our shoulders as we did our satchel. Later, as the cardboard boxes got torn and tattered, special gas mask covers made from waterproof materials were for sale in the shops.

My mother made us new covers when Grandma took an old leather covered settee to pieces. She borrowed a sewing machine, cut out the covers from the best of the leather, stitched them up and put a large snap pop on the front, they looked as good as some of the new ones my school friends had got.

Once a week we had gas mask practice. The teachers went round checking that each child's mask fitted properly. I hated this because I suffered from claustrophobia and always thought I might suffocate with my gas mask on. Usually I ended up gasping, dripping with perspiration and the visor so fogged up I couldn't see out.

Recently, I had got into the habit of muttering the Lord's Prayer to myself, over and over again, every time the siren went. Praying there would be no gas. I was convinced I would be one of the first to die, knowing I wouldn't be able to keep my gas mask on long enough to survive.

My father was in his element these days, busy telling everyone about gas, what a terrible thing it was, what it had done to him and his mates during the war. 'Look what it did to me' he declared. 'I can't work, if I'd had a gas mask like you in those days, I'd be a healthy man today. Take heed what I say, always take your gas mask with you.' He was a fine one to talk I thought, I'd never seen him take his anywhere, nor could I ever remember him fitting it on.

He really put the wind up me one day, I overheard him talking to grandma and one or two of her friends. 'Watch out for the smell of mustard,' he was saying. 'It could be mustard gas. Get yourselves indoors quick, shut your doors and windows. It's a wicked chemical gas. Where it touches your skin it brings up huge blisters. But the worst thing is if you breathe it in, it burns your lungs, huge blisters develop inside you and you die.'

I wasn't sure if father was pulling their legs or not, but the ladies shivered in horror. Being a nervous little 8 year old, it put the wind up me too. For weeks after that I always sniffed when I went outside the door, to see if I could smell mustard.

One day I did an unforgivable thing. I overslept, got up and dashed straight off to school without my gas mask. I was sent home to fetch it. Told not to waste any time but to run all the way there, then all the way back to school, so I didn't miss very much of my lesson. After all it was only just over a mile. When I returned puffing and panting, and covered in perspiration, I had to stand out in front of the class. Then as an example to the other children not to forget their gas masks, I received two slaps on each hand with a wooden ruler.

A dug out or air- raid shelter had now been completed on the playing field at the back of the school. Now if the siren sounded, we had to file quickly out of the building, cross the playground into the playing field, then down the steps to the shelter. Once there we sat on the wooden benches provided and kept as quiet as possible so the teachers could hear when the All Clear sounded.

The first time this happened I was so excited. Being down in the dugout meant no lessons, or so I thought. However things didn't turn out quite like that. 'If you think you have come down here to sit idle,' roared the teacher, 'then you can all think again. You'll work just as hard down here, if not harder.' The teacher waved the ruler at us. She never forgot to take that with her.

One day after a lengthy spell of doing tables and spellings, the teachers got worried. They had been listening hard for the All Clear to sound but they had not heard it. We had been down in the shelter for two and a half hours and it was time for us to go home.

Had it gone and we hadn't heard it? argued one teacher as she walked to the steps to look round. There was no gunfire now, no aeroplanes flying round to break the silence, so satisfied she returned. 'We shall have to risk it' she said. So in orderly fashion we filed out of the shelter and into school, grabbed our coats and hats and dashed home as fast as we could. Just as we reached home we heard the All Clear sounding.

Next day it was decided that the top of our shelter should be camouflaged, as the freshly dug earth from above must appear very conspicuous. We had an hour or so outside raking it all level so it looked like flower beds, we even planted seeds and plants on it.

I awoke one night to hear whispers, slipped out of bed and discovered my mother and sister kneeling beside the open bedroom window. Thinking there was an air raid and they hadn't wakened me I began to ask questions. 'Quiet,' they hushed, 'we have a midnight visitor.' It was black outside. We could not see a thing, not even each other inside. I could hear the sound of a bicycle being wheeled along, as somebody tramped round and round in my father's garden.

This amused me. I almost burst out laughing, for he had only dug it that afternoon. Childlike I felt it was a way of getting back at him, for 'squaring me up' as he had called it earlier in the day.

A toneless voice now began singing, 'Daisy, Daisy, give me your answer do. Oh blast me.' A little more tramping around and the voice started up once more. 'When Irish eyes are smiling, sure tis like the froth on my beer.' Bicycle and midnight visitor sat down with a thump. My mother stifled a chuckle,

'I know who that is.' she whispered. 'It's Wally Hawkins, I recognise the voice. I heard he was home on leave. Reckon he's been down to the pub to celebrate. Though what he is doing round this way I can't imagine. He lives at the other end of the village. On his way home, being probably plastered, he's taken the wrong road and ended up here.'

With a loud audible grunt and a muttered 'Oh dear me,' our mysterious visitor appeared to rise to his feet and pick up the bicycle, wheel it from the garden onto the path and stand under our window. We still could not see him but we could sense that he was there.

Mother whispered in my ear. 'Don't make a sound, but if you can go quietly and fetch the glass of water from beside your bed, bring it here.' Upon my return she took it from me and carefully leaned out of the window and poured it over whoever was beneath us.

From below came a startled exclamation. 'Blast me, it's starting to rain! Somehow I don't think I live here, so I'd better be going and finding out where I do live before I get any wetter,' and off he went. We don't know where he spent the night, but early next morning he was seen pedalling homewards. We laughed about it for days and whenever we saw him after that, we told mother she was a good shot. She chuckled and replied,
'You've always got to be ready for anything, for you never know what's going to happen out here in the country.'

We didn't know much about cars. There were only three in the whole village. The village shopkeeper had a van and there were one or two motor bikes with sidecar attached. So we were not in the least worried when we heard petrol was being rationed. My mother said it would be hard for those who relied on their car for their living, or business to keep going on a miserable petrol allowance, but petrol wasn't the only worry. All sorts of rules and regulations had now come into force.

We knew from personal experience how difficult it was to find our way around in the black-out. It must have been worse for the motorist with their masked headlights. No light was allowed inside your car, or the use of a wireless if there was one. The bumpers and running boards that cars had in those days had to be painted white.

A speed of only twenty miles an hour was allowed after dark and it amazed me how with those hooded lights, they could see to get a long at all. If we were out after dark and heard a car coming, we usually did the wise and sensible thing and got up on a bank out of the way. For us children at night a car resembled a roaring, spluttering monster.

If you parked your car in a garage or locked shed, you were alright, but if it was parked outside your house in the roadway, you were supposed to immobilize it in some manner, so it couldn't be driven away. Meaning of course, if the Germans should be parachuted in. Petrol rations didn't go as far as people hoped, and according to the tales we heard drivers were desperate to go to any lengths to make it go further.

We roared with laughter when a neighbour told us about an acquaintance of his who added paraffin to his petrol. Apparently the car had gone off up the road like a rocket, backfiring all the way and with clouds of black smoke billowing out from its exhaust.

All the signposts had now been removed, to confuse the Germans, should they land. We children got quite excited about this and told our mothers we could no longer attend school as we didn't know which way to go. Unfortunately this excuse didn't work and we still had to go.

Food rationing had been in force for some time now, everyone having been supplied with a ration book. It had started with ham and bacon, then sugar, butter and meat. tea came next which hit some people really hard, for it was only two ounces per week for each person. It didn't go very far, I remember my mother opening the tea packet and shaking out every last little tealeaf.

When invited in for a cup of tea, you never knew what to expect. For people resorted to all sorts of ways to preserve their precious tea supply. Some pots being emptied only once a day, for every fresh brew a further teaspoonful of tea was added. Others drained the teapot out and the next time they wanted tea they heated the left over liquid up in a saucepan. Two ounces of lard and four of margarine were now added to the list of rationed items, then cheese. One ounce per person. When my mother put my father's cheese ration in front of him, he said 'What's that, bait for the mousetrap?'

Sausages had not been rationed. The problem was to get hold of them. When they did arrive in the shops, there seemed to be an instant queue lined up to buy them. Sometimes people would queue for hours, then just as you got to the counter the shopkeeper would say, 'Sorry sold out' what a disappointment.

If you were one of the lucky ones who had managed to buy some sausages, you never knew what was inside them. Perhaps it was better not to know. Some were filled with horrible red meat and looked revolting. Others varied in colour, some so pale looking as if they were filled with nothing else but breadcrumbs.

Grandfather would laugh as he cut his sausage in half, and say 'I never know what I'm going to need with my sausage, a drop of mustard or to spread it with jam.'
Grandma's answer would be, 'Think yourself lucky you've got a sausage, lots of poor people haven't.'

Our grandparents lived close by. We were over there one evening as grandfather was getting ready to go out. Although he had been at work all day and was tired, it made no difference to your war jobs. If you had a meeting to attend or were on duty you had to go.

After he had departed, we stayed to keep grandma company for a while, before going back home. Barely had we got inside the door of our house when my sister Jean shouted 'I can hear the siren, it's the warning, I can hear another one in the distance.' Immediately guns along the coast began firing. Then came the sound of the aeroplanes.

The oil lamp that had just been lit was hastily extinguished. Everywhere was in darkness. 'Are you all here?' my mother asked. 'then quick, get under the table.' An enemy plane roared overhead, followed by another and yet another, they seemed continuous. Grinding along with their loads of bombs, as if it was all they could do to get along. I was terrified, as I always was during an air raid and shook with fright. 'Stay under the table' ordered my mother, 'I'm going outside to take a look.'

Mother left the door ajar and soon my two sisters wriggled out and went to join her. I was too scared to sit all alone, so followed them. Mother was busy peering up into the night sky. 'I think I see one of them, well not see it, but I can just make out a very faint glow from his exhaust.'

Suddenly up shot a long beam of light, it was quite bright and close by. 'It's our searchlight,' shouted my sister Jean enthusiastically as she jumped up and down. If I hadn't been so frightened, it would have been exciting watching that powerful beam of light probing up into the darkness to find the hostile aircraft. Another searchlight shot up to join it, making an arc across the sky. There right at the very tips of their beams we glimpsed a tiny speck of silver.

The enemy aircraft twisted and turned in it's endeavour to escape, but the searchlight crews were clever and well trained. They managed to hold it. And the guns began firing upwards. The outcome was inevitable. A terrific flash of light, followed a few seconds later by a gigantic explosion. 'Cor,' muttered my younger sister Eliza, her hands held over her ears. 'We did it didn't we? We blew it to smithereens.'

There came a lull now. The searchlights had disappeared, though we could still hear faint bangs and flashes in the distance. Some twenty minutes later the raiders began returning, roaring back over our house towards the coast. Seeming to be in so much more of a hurry now they had disposed of their loads. Just when we thought they had all gone, we heard another one approaching. It was making a peculiar noise, the engine popping and banging, occasionally cutting out all together.

'Oh my God!' cried my mother, sounding extremely agitated, as indeed she was. 'Inside quick.' We didn't need telling twice, before she finished speaking we were racing for the door. Soon we were huddled together like sardines in a can.

A terrific explosion shook the air. The house shook on its foundations.

The windows rattled. I thought the glass would shatter. Pheasants in the nearby wood and fields called out in terror. There came another explosion, 'He's coming closer.' whispered my mother anxiously. 'I think he must have been hit before he could find his target and is now jettisoning his bomb load.'

Another far louder explosion was heard. A brilliant flash came right through the black-out curtains. 'Wonder if he has got any more on board,' whispered my sister Jean, 'or will he crash right on us, he sounds pretty rough.'

'Keep going, keep going; please keep going' moaned Eliza.'I've got my fingers crossed.' I think we all had sitting there under the table listening.
'God be with us.' prayed my mother. 'If it's our turn to go, let it be quick, don't let us suffer.'
'Amen,' came my sister's voice from the darkness.

I listened to my family talking, but was too frightened to do or say anything. My heart thudded in my chest until I thought it might burst. My limbs shook uncontrollably. My teeth chattered. I felt powerless to stop them, seeming to have no control over myself at all.

Slowly, so dreadfully, painfully slowly, the plane groaned and laboured above us, while we winced in anticipation of another bomb. Any minute, I thought, we will all be blown to Kingdom Come. And that will be the end of us. Surprisingly our luck held. Gradually the plane seemed to be pulling away.

'I think we are safe,' came my mother's relieved voice, 'If he had another bomb to drop I feel sure he would have dropped it by now.' 'I think he's on fire,' she muttered. 'There seems to be a small flickering glow in the sky, yet I can't think he's too badly damaged or he wouldn't be trying to get home. I bet those poor lads on board are frightened to death, wondering if they are going to see their loved ones again.'

Then up started the anti aircraft guns that were posted along the coast. 'They are firing at him,' my sister cried excitedly, scrambling out from beneath the table to join my mother, 'I do hope they get him.' They were unlucky, the last we heard and saw, was a faint glow in the sky and the rapidly fading roar of the engines. Then and only then did I crawl out to join the rest of my family and to realise that I was wet all round my rear end.

'That blooming old cat!' I shouted indignantly, 'It must have weed under the table and I've been and sat in it.' Instead of getting the sympathy I thought I deserved, the family roared with laughter. 'Oh do stop blaming the poor cat,' cried Jean scathingly, 'be honest and say, you were so frightened you wet yourself.'

Next morning we were up bright and early and set off to see where the bombs had dropped. They had been spread out over several fields, not very far away. We were not the only ones looking. It seemed half the village was there, standing around and studying the huge craters. 'War,' declared an elderly woman, as she leaned heavily on her walking stick. 'is an evil and wicked thing. What a blessing those bombs fell where they could do no harm. Had he begun dropping them a few seconds later they would have fallen on the village and a lot of us standing here today might have been killed. We have a lot to be thankful for.'

Hardly a day went by now without the siren sounding, mornings and afternoons, but more often than not it was in the evenings. Especially if the weather was fine, or the sky was moonlit. The only time we could really relax was if it snowed or poured with rain. Then the Germans wouldn't send their planes over, because the heavy clouds would obscure their targets.

My father would never get up if there was an air raid at night. 'What's the use,' he would say, 'if I am going to die, I might as well die in the comfort of my bed.' Our next door neighbour Annie was crippled by arthritis and lived alone. If the siren sounded during the evening and the air raid was bad and frightened her, she would bang on the wall and we would go round to sit with her.

I was always scared when we did this. As soon as we were out of the door, I ran like the wind round the corner and in at her door. I always felt the German Planes flying overhead could see me and might drop something on me.

We never knew how long an air raid would last. Sometimes it was all over in half an hour, other times it lasted several hours. Many times we have sat with our neighbour until well into the early hours of the morning. I kept awake the whole of the time, listening and straining my ears for the next plane. My elder sister used to lay on Annie's couch and doze. Sometimes Jean fell into such a deep sleep that she was left there all night.

These days there was a shortage of coal. With long delayed deliveries, we were lucky if we saw the coalman once in three months. Even then you couldn't have as much as you wanted, only what he allowed you to have. It was no use burning it up straight away. You had to eke it out very carefully because you never knew when he would be coming again.

The winter was so cold, people burned everything they could lay their hands on: old furniture, wood, pine cones, books and occasionally old footwear. In fact anything and everything that would burn and help save the coal and bring a little warmth into the house.

Many people discovered that as their coal got low, they had piles of coal dust remaining. Desperate to use it up we heard that a few people were experimenting. Mixing cement powder with their coal dust, they added a little water and fashioned it into cakes or bricks. When dried it was supposed to burn very well. We never tried it, we didn't have much coal dust, my mother used ours a little bit at a time.

We only had a cooking range. This was for cooking and heating. Rather than let the fire go out over night or when she was out, my mother saved all her vegetable peelings and tea leaves and damped the fire down with those. It used to smoke and sizzle at first but was quite effective.

One winter it was so bitterly cold, we went to bed each night with a little stone hot water bottle. It wasn't really a hot water bottle, but a stone ginger beer bottle filled with hot water. It helped keep us warm. According to my mother you couldn't buy hot water bottles for love nor money.

A school chum told us her mother put bricks in the oven or stood them on top of the stove during the evening. By bedtime they were nicely hot. She then placed them in the beds to take the chill off. Their poor grandfather who lived with them, forgot to take his out and rammed his feet down the bed and broke two of his toes. They said he was off work for six weeks.

With all the rationing things were pretty grim and, now they were getting worse. We had to have coupons for tinned foods, fish, treacle, fruit, marmalade and jams, tinned meats, beans and soups. On top of everything else we also had clothing coupons. At the start everyone was to receive 66 coupons each a year. Different items of clothing needed different amounts of coupons. My mother did not use all of her coupons she passed them over to friends in exchange for outgrown cast off children's clothes. She had no money herself and this way she provided more clothes for us children.

Coupons were also issued for sweets. The allowance per person was eight ounces a month, two ounces a week. It didn't go very far. When we noticed the sweet man's van standing outside the village shop. We grabbed coupons and money and stood waiting for him to leave.

Before the shopkeeper had had time to unpack everything we were there at the door to buy our monthly supply before they ran out. There wasn't much variety; butter crunch or mint imperials, extra strong mints or humbugs and occasionally toffees. There was chocolate too, but we preferred sweets, thinking that they lasted longer. Over the next few hours we'd suck and chew and champ until our monthly sweet ration was all gone and all we had left was the memory.

Registration cards had now been issued. This was a folded card with our names and address printed on it and a number. Everyone had one and by law all adults were supposed to carry theirs around with them. Anyone could be asked to produce it at any time. Failure to do so could mean a fine.

Although we wanted to, our parents wouldn't allow us to carry ours around with us, in case they were lost. So we had to learn our number off by heart. Mine was TXJC 274, my sisters one above and one below mine. We were so proud of our number that at school we played a little game where we called ourselves by our numbers rather than our names. It was like being in the Secret Service or something similar. 'Hullo TXJC 274.' 'Hullo TXJC 298,' and so it went on. Woe betide anyone who could not remember their number.

One morning my mother was almost out of her mind with worry. She had lost or misplaced one of our precious ration books. Remembering that she had last used it when shopping in the store in the next village, she made a frantic dash over there on her bicycle to inquire.

'No,' she was told she hadn't left it there, nor had it been handed in. It was unlikely to be, with food in short supply anyone finding a ration book would be sorely tempted to hang onto it, especially if it had any coupons left in it.

Upon her return the house was searched from top to bottom, cushions pulled off chairs, drawers turned out, coat pockets, handbag and shopping bags, but there was no sign of the elusive ration book.

Now this was very serious. The book was needed at the weekend when the grocer made his delivery. The only thing my mother could think to do was to catch the next bus over to Lowestoft, dash along to the Food Office, explain what had happened, hope they replaced it and then catch the next bus home.

Now going to Lowestoft these days was a dangerous business. There had been so many air raids recently. Often daylight raids. Buildings had been bombed and people killed. Just supposing, I thought, there was another air raid while my mother was there? I tried to persuade her not to go, frightened for her safety, until my sister Jean mentioned I would have to starve. It was my ration book that was missing.

With her mind made up, mother hastily began to get ready. Then grandma came. 'If you are going to catch that bus' she grumbled, 'you'll have to hurry, it goes in five minutes, unless your clock is wrong.' Straight out of the door dashed mother. Grabbing her bike she pedalled off as fast as her legs would go. It was nearly a mile to the bus stop. As she arrived the bus was already coming along the road. She flagged it down. As it slowed she pushed her bike behind a hedge and got on the bus.

I was on tenterhooks the whole time, sitting outside listening in case the siren went. Then Jean who had been left in charge, suggested I walk down to the corner and meet the bus. It would give me something to do and think about.

I agreed, but didn't walk. I ran all the way, checked to make sure my mother's bicycle was there behind the hedge, then sat down on the bank nearby and waited impatiently. I hadn't heard the siren I thought, but that wasn't to say it hadn't gone off. The wind might be in the wrong direction. What if there had been an air raid and bombs dropped, supposing one had fallen on the Food Office when my mother was inside?

I was so worried and lost in my thoughts that I pulled a whole clump of grass into tiny fragments, not noticing the bus coming until it drew up with a squeal of brakes. My mother stepped off. Hardly able to contain my delight I stood up and shouted jubilantly. 'Were you able to get me a new ration book?'

'Yes no trouble at all,' came the reply. 'I've had a most enjoyable time, everywhere I went people smiled at me, stopped for a word or two or said 'good morning.' People on the bus, along the street and even in the Food Office. You would have thought I was royalty, ever so friendly they were. When I left they saw me to the door and stood laughing and waving until I was out of sight, real nice people they couldn't have treated me better.'

We found out why as we walked back home, she was wearing a black shoe on one foot and a red old fashioned styled shoe with a very pointed toe on the other. Previously one of great auntie's cast off's. Plus one black stocking and one a light grey colour with a large hole near the ankle from which ran a very wide ladder all the way up the back!

Chapter 3 Careless Talk

We still carried our gas masks around with us. They made useful weapons when the boys had an argument or fight. They would whip them off their shoulders and whirl them round by the strap with no thought for the consequences. Often they struck their opponent, other times it was the road. When we had gas mask practice many of their masks had huge dents in the bottom. They didn't worry, they still worked they said, the only thing was they looked a bit peculiar.

There was a little ditty running round the school these days which we sang over and over again. It went, 'Underneath the spreading chestnut tree. Old Neville Chamberlain said to me. If you want to get your gas mask free,' then everyone would shout at the top of their voices, 'join the blooming ARP.'

We now had a name tag each to wear round our necks with our names and addresses. This was in case the school was bombed and there were dead or injured children. It would help to identify us. Proper ones that hung on a chain round your neck could now be bought, if you had the money but most of us were poor. Postcards were bought and cut into four, your name and address written on it, a hole made and a piece of fine string threaded through and tied round the neck.

My mother helped occasionally in the village shop and brought home fine elastic that had held tubes of glue and ointment to a cardboard backing. She also found transparent paper. Writing our names on the card, she covered it with transparent paper, threaded the fine elastic through and tied it round our necks. We slept with these on, just in case we were late up in the morning and forgot them. For to go to school without them could mean trouble with our teachers. I had never forgotten what happened when I went to school without my gas mask. I had no wish to feel that ruler in action again.

For a long time now we had been having lectures at school about the dangers of careless talk. We were warned if our fathers, brothers or uncles came home on leave, it was advisable not to say, if we knew of course, which ship they were on, where they were stationed, or if on embarkation leave and going abroad.

Just in case anyone was listening and it got to the ears of a German spy. They would then have an idea where our troops were, or which ships were in port and where. Or where our troops were being sent to.

'Careless talk,' said our teachers 'cost lives.' Posters to that effect were stuck up on notice boards, in shops, streets and bus stations, even on the buses themselves. Anywhere where people would see and notice them. There were other posters too, besides careless talk. The most popular ones being, 'Walls have Ears,' 'Keep it under your Hat' and 'be like Father, Keep Mum.'

We children took all these things seriously. Now if we wanted to tell our friends our father, brother, or uncle were home, we'd look all around us making sure nobody was within hearing distance, before whispering what we wanted to say. We also viewed strangers with the utmost suspicion.

One day, on our way home from school, we met a man dressed all in black and wearing a 'dog collar' so we presumed he was a parson, vicar or something to do with the church. He smiled, said he was lost and please could we help him. He had a message for a Mrs Smith or was it Brown, who lived in either Ash Tree Lane or was it Oak Tree Lane, he wasn't certain. First he said one and then the other. He spoke different too, as if he didn't come from around these parts.

Now there were only two or three people who lived in Oak Tree Lane. We children knew every one who lived there. We never heard of Ash Tree Lane. The only Smith in the village was my aunt who lived next door to grandma. We didn't know of any Browns, never heard of any. About to open my mouth and say so I was rudely shoved aside by older boys who immediately began directing this gentleman in completely the wrong direction.

I was most indignant. As the poor man walked away thanking us profusely. 'Why did you tell him that way.' I muttered angrily. 'You know it's a lie.'

'Be quiet and use your eyes and ears,' one of the boys snapped, 'surely you could see he was an old Jerry spy. Two or three times he forgot himself and said 'Ja.' 'He knew by asking for Smith or Brown he was fairly safe, they are two of the most common names you can find.'

I was shocked and lost no time in dashing home to tell mother all about the queer-looking parson we had seen and what the boys had said about him. 'Might be advisable to just mention it to your grandfather when he comes home from work' she said, 'but wait until he has had his tea, It does sound peculiar.'

Before I could do so great aunty popped in to see us. She was on her way home after visiting a friend. As she cycled along she had noticed this strange looking man of the cloth, hurrying along Oak Tree Lane. We immediately told her we had seen him to. He had spoken to us, asking about Mrs Smith or Mrs Brown.

'I'm the only Smith in the village' spluttered auntie indignantly. 'He couldn't have been looking for me. I don't like the sound of it, not one little bit.' We talked it over, then all went across to see grandfather. He heard us out, then thought it important enough to notify the police. Although they kept an eye out for our parson he was not seen again.

A few months later our cousins came to stay with grandma. They lived about 30 miles away. Talking one evening, we mentioned the queer looking parson that we had seen and thought was a spy. They were extremely interested, their father was a member of the ARP. He had mentioned to their mother about arresting a man acting suspiciously. He had been dressed as a parson. When searched, they found plans of airfields, gun positions and last but not least a plan of the searchlight based in the woods, at the very bottom of Oak Tree Lane.

Nearly every night there were air raids. Some nights they were worse than others. Quite late one night German planes kept continually flying over. We did not get much sleep and sat in our usual place huddled under the table. As the enemy planes began returning it became obvious one or two of them had bombs left.

When the first bang came, my mother gasped. 'Good Lord that was close.' Then came a couple more bangs, and after a few seconds an almighty explosion. The windows rattled, the whole house shook, even the brick floor I was sitting on seemed to shake. As soon as it became quieter outside, my mother was off to look around. She always said that if somebody had been hurt she might be able to help.

Next morning we heard two bombs had dropped on the lawns and greenhouses belonging to a large house nearby, another into a field where two horses grazed; fortunately neither was injured. On our way to school we stopped to look at the big crater in the field. It looked enormous. We stood on the edge gazing in awe into its depth. I thought if one bomb can make a hole this size, what would it have done to our house if it had struck that? There would have been nothing left.

Quite often incendiary bombs were also dropped. These caused fires, which were usually soon put out and didn't cause a lot of harm unless they happened to fall in a field of ripe corn or something of that sort. The Home Guard based in the Rectory usually helped to deal with those.

A woman had been going round the village recently visiting all the houses, asking if any one had any spare rooms. They were evacuating children from London and other big towns because of the bad air raids and wanted accommodation for them. We hadn't any room, but the woman insisted in coming in and seeing for herself.

Our neighbour had room, but had to get a letter from her doctor to say she couldn't look after evacuees because of her arthritis. Weeks passed and people forgot about them, then suddenly out of the blue the evacuees had arrived. At school strange - talking children were in our classroom. Most of them were homesick, missing their parents and friends, their shops and their way of life. They didn't like the country, the school or the teachers nor us, it was all so different to them. After a week or two they gradually left and went back home.

Head lice soon became rife. Almost every child in the school was infected. My mother was devastated when we began scratching. Out came the paraffin jar. After soaking our hair with it, it was left for fifteen minutes before being rinsed. The paraffin killed the lice but left our hair so full of oil it needed three or four washes with soapflakes before it was anywhere near back to normal.

'Those evacuees brought that scourge down with them,' it was said. 'We never had that in the school before they came.' Scarlatina followed, then itches between the fingers and toes, Chicken Pox and finally Measles. All were blamed on the evacuees.

My sister Jean had Measles first. Confined to bed for a few days she worried my parents silly because she wouldn't eat. Several of the neighbours sent around or brought little titbits, hoping to tempt her appetite. It was hopeless, but she did seem to be better so she was allowed downstairs for an hour or so, while mother drew back the curtains, opened the window and changed the sheets on the bed. Mopping round the floor she found a mountain of apple cores under the bed. Having a good crop of apples this year and no outhouses to put them in, they were laid out under the beds. All my sister was doing when she felt hungry was reaching under the bed for another apple.

A couple of weeks later my younger sister and I came out in spots. We only had a mild attack but we had dreadful coughs and colds. We were recovering and over the worst when one evening the siren went. As usual the anti aircraft guns along the coast began firing and the roar of approaching enemy planes was heard. Soon they were roaring overhead.

Hastily the lamp was extinguished. 'Under the table quick' ordered my mother. We didn't really need telling, Eliza and I were already there. Jean refused to sit next to me these days
'In case' she would say with a grin, 'the old cat has been and I don't want to get wet.'

The guns kept up their incessant racket. Then came the explosions. Windows rattled, the floor heaved, I pressed both hands over my ears. More detonations followed, nearly deafening us. In the midst of it all came a loud persistent knocking on the wall. It was our neighbour's signal. 'That sounds like Annie' muttered my mother. She's frightened, poor soul and all alone, I must go round.'

'You children had better not come with your coughs and colds, I'll go and explain why we can't stay with her.'
'Don't go round there'. I pleaded as another plane roared overhead. 'You might get hit with something. It sounds bad out there.'
'I know it does she stated 'but you three have got each other, poor Annie has got nobody'.

I thought how brave my mother was. Nothing would have induced me to go outside tonight, not even to run next door. Another enemy plane came roaring over and from the distance more gunfire, bangs and flashes. Sitting there with my two sisters I was as usual shaking with fright. 'Can you hear that old Rattlesnake?' teased my sister Eliza. It was my teeth chattering.

The knocking from next door had ceased so we guessed my mother had arrived. The next plane that went over seemed so low, we thought it was going to sit down on the roof of the house. After what seemed an age, we heard voices outside, someone fumbled for the door handle, then it opened. 'Here we are girls' came my mothers voice. 'As you are not fit enough to go round and sit with Annie, I've brought her around to be with us. We are both safe and sound.'

As she spoke, a brilliant flash came right through the open door, followed by a mighty crack, then another. 'Oh my God,' shrieked Annie, crippled though she was with arthritis she released my mother's arm she had been leaning on, flung herself down and crawled under the table to join us. There she lay for she couldn't sit up, the table wasn't tall enough and both her legs stuck out at one end.

'Quick!' we shouted to my mother as another explosion came. 'Get under here with us.' Mother was busy pulling a big armchair over, resting it against the table so that it covered Annie's legs.

'There, that should help if we get a direct hit,' she muttered, as she finally crawled in beside us.

A direct hit? I immediately panicked, that would be the end of everything. I don't want to die yet. I wanted to live, to grow up and become a woman and be like lots of other people and enjoy my life. As my thoughts ran on everyone else was silent, probably if I did but know, their thoughts were running along the same lines as my own.

Still breathing heavily after her exertions, Annie who was a well built woman finally broke the silence. 'Them damn German planes are still coming over, don't seem as if they are ever going to stop. Have you noticed it's getting lighter outside, almost as if the moon is up?'

'I have' replied my mother, 'It's been worrying me. There shouldn't be any moon tonight.'
'What else can it be?' declared Annie, 'It can't be a fire can it? the colour isn't right.'

'I know,' burst out my young sister, 'we all fell asleep and didn't remember it. Now we have woken up again and it's morning, the sun is shining and it's going to be a nice day.'
'In that case I had better get up and see,' mumbled my mother, beginning to edge herself backwards from under the table.

'Have you noticed,' she said to Annie, 'how those planes come over, then veer to the left? They are all going the same way tonight, almost as if they know exactly where to go. Something serious is going on out there, I think and I want to now what it is.' Amidst our calls to be careful she crept over to the window, pulling aside a corner of the blackout curtain. Immediately a shaft of light shone in, she lifted the curtain higher, it was like daylight outside. 'Can't see what's causing it, I'm going outside to take a look.'

As the door opened I peered out from under the table and was amazed. I could see the garden clearly, my mother's flowers, father's sprout plants standing to attention in a neat row across the garden, his tomatoes hanging on the plants everything was so vivid.

Stepping warily out, my mother looked around and saw in the sky right over the house a huge light like an artificial moon. As the German planes had ceased to pass overhead, she called us out to have a look. I only dared to go as far as the door, but my elder sister was more brave. Soon she was standing beside my mother gazing in wonder at the phenomenon in the sky.

The light burned for another hour, gradually growing dimmer. Finally it appeared to break in two and drift apart. When the All Clear finally sounded, we found we had a difficult task ahead of us getting our neighbour to her feet.

First the table was lifted from over her, so she could sit up. Then my mother and sister took hold of her hands and pulled with all their might. Annie was such a heavy weight, her bottom lifted from the floor then dropped back. Time and time again they tried until my mother looked exhausted. 'I give up,' she finally said, 'I think what I had better do, is to go out and see if I can find somebody to come and help otherwise you are going to be sitting there all night.'

The prospect looked grim, I who hadn't helped, suggested we try once more. I picked up the poker from the hearth. 'When I wave this for the third time,' I told them, 'you all pull, I'll drop the poker and push from behind.' They weren't very keen but to oblige me, they agreed.

'One, two, three.' I said as they began to pull, slowly Annie's bottom began to rise from the floor, instead of dropping the poker as planned and helping to push, I jabbed her hard with it. Instantly with a shriek she shot to her feet. While Annie rubbed her backside ruefully, we all fell about laughing. What a lovely ending to our traumatic experience.

Next morning on the lawn of a big house around the corner was found a huge parachute. It was said to be as big as a circus marquee. It was thought to have been part of whatever had suspended an enormous marker flare in the sky.

Crockery was hard to find these days, as not much was being made. Woe betide anyone careless enough to break anything. I broke a cup one day and was afraid to tell my mother, so I hid the pieces away. She knew one was missing and searched high and low. The trouble was I'd broken one the week before too. When I told her she had cried. I was so afraid of upsetting her again. I was found out eventually and had my bottom smacked for not owning up.

Saucepans and frying pans were difficult to get, as were teapots. When the end of our spout got knocked off, all we could get was a rubber spout to put on the end of it. It took ages to fit and even then it leaked.

Matches were also scarce at this time. We used paper spills to light the lamp from the stove, if a small spark could be nurtured in the fire in the mornings, to save using a precious match then my mother was happy.

Father wasn't happy when he couldn't get his tobacco which was in short supply. He was bad tempered and snappy with everyone. He paced up and down the garden path, muttering to himself about bloody old Hitler, who was to blame for everything, My mother told him to be quiet and if he paced up and down many more times he'd fall through to Australia.

Most shopkeepers kept their limited supply of tobacco for their regular customers. There were stories of men getting desperate and mixing various leaves, herbs and grasses with their tobacco to make it go further. Father made us laugh when he told us of an acquaintance of his who cut up an assortment of various substances with a pair of scissors. When satisfied it was cut fine enough he rolled it up in a cigarette paper, then offered it to father. 'I'm glad I declined' he said, 'for when the old boy lit it, the flame ran all the way up the side and singed one side of his moustache.'

A neighbour managed to get hold of some tobacco plants. He gave some to father who was as pleased as punch. He tended them carefully, dried the leaves when they were big enough, storing it all away to mature in cocoa tins. He left it several weeks but when he got it out to use he found it had all gone mouldy.

We had what was called War Savings Week, during which events were organised for the whole week. There would be a fete somewhere in the village, sometimes two on different days. Then perhaps a dance or social, a whist drive or sale. Anything that would raise money for the war effort.

As we left school on Friday, we were asked to bring sixpence to buy a savings stamp on the following Monday. If we did it would entitle us to have a ride on a Bren gun carrier. My problem was where to get a sixpence from. My father having been gassed, meant he wasn't fit enough to get a job and work, the family only had a very small income and there were three of us at school.

I did so want a ride like the other children. I heard them talking so confidently about getting sixpence, that I felt quite envious. However on Sunday, I ran half a mile to post an urgent letter for a neighbour, when I got back she gave me tuppence.

In the afternoon Grandma needed a hand picking raspberry leaves so she could make someone a lotion for spots and pimples. Grandma gave me another tuppence. After tea great auntie popped in for a few minutes, as she left she found a few coppers in her pocket and gave us a penny each for our money box.

I counted my tuppences and my penny. If I did not put it in my money box I would have one, two, three, four, five pennies towards my Bren Gun Carrier ride. I felt quite rich as I repeatedly counted it, hoping and praying that the next time it would make six not five. Then as if from Heaven a penny dropped on the table beside me and someone shouted 'six.'

Startled I looked up and saw Jean's grinning face. 'It's only lent,' she declared, 'not given. You can pay me back sometime.' I was so grateful for the loan but I can't remember to this day whether I ever paid her back.

My mother took my coppers next morning and put me a silver sixpence in a twist of newspaper, which I clutched firmly in my hand as I made my way to school. I was so relieved when I finally handed it to the teacher and knew it was safe.

Wednesday the day of the ride dawned. We ran to school in great excitement. We were so inattentive at our lessons, the teacher threatened to cancel the Bren Gun Carrier rides. After eating our sandwiches at midday, we were sent out into the playground, but nobody played. We stood around miserably wondering if the teacher would keep her word.

Presently, however she appeared and opened the school gates wide. Then we knew everything was all right. Soon we heard the roar we had been waiting for, nearer and nearer it came then through the gates swept two Bren Gun Carriers.

They drove around in a circle, their tracks throwing up mud and grit. Immediately they came and stopped in front of the door, we all surged forward. Bren Gun Carriers often passed us on the road, but we had never been this close to one before. The teachers shouted at us, 'Keep back children, keep back.' It was like talking to a brick wall, we paid not the slightest attention.

There were two soldiers in each carrier. After getting out and conferring with the teachers, a few names were called out and those children helped aboard. Off they went laughing, shouting and waving goodbye. Some mothers had now arrived to see the fun and stood around talking.

We anxiously awaited the carriers' return. They seemed to have been gone a long while. They were back and gone again before it was finally my turn. I was lifted on by somebody's mum, passed to a soldier who sat me on a hard metal bench seat. As soon as we were full we set off, waving and shouting as the others had done to everyone left behind in the playground.

It was sheer bliss, but a little bit scary. We went quite slowly along the road, then turned off along a rugged track that lead to an area of marshy common land. Now we picked up speed and fairly tore along up a hill and down the other side, so fast it felt I'd left my stomach behind. We headed straight for a bush and when I thought we would swerve to avoid it we went right over the top of it. Then through the middle of a great big one dividing it in two.

Our driver then attempted to cross a dyke and appeared to have got stuck halfway. 'Now look what you've done' he admonished us, 'You'll all have to get out and push, or we will be here all night.' He was only pulling our legs, for he shot the carrier into reverse and out we came. After turning in a circle, he went at it full speed and through we went, water cascading in the air and coming down all over us.
The soldiers roared with laughter, for they knew what would happen, 'Did you like that?' called the driver.
'Yes' shrieked the boys,
'No' squealed the girls. Nonetheless he took us through it again. He spun us around in circles until we felt dizzy, up the hill again and down the other side, then we tore across the heath at breakneck speed, through a hedge and down a steep bank, during which we girls had our eyes shut, thinking we were about to turn over, then we were on the road and driving slowly and sedately back to school.

I enjoyed my ride so much, I didn't want to remove myself from the carrier when it was over, but other children were eagerly waiting to take our places. I noticed my mother had arrived and was chatting to her friends, then grandma who had been cycling past, stopped to watch the fun.

At the very end the teacher said, 'Everyone has now had their ride, but these kind gentlemen,' she pointed to the soldiers, 'have assured me, they have time to do one more trip each. If any one would like to pay sixpence to buy another savings stamp, you may have another ride.' I watched enviously as mothers put their hands in their pockets and children ran forward. Feeling a hand grasp my shoulder, I turned and there stood grandma holding out a sixpence. I grabbed it and ran to take the last place. I was so happy as I set off, thinking what a lucky girl I was, I hadn't thought even to have had the chance of one ride in the beginning and now I'd have two.

My mother and her friend had been attending first aid classes, held in a room at the Rectory on Saturday afternoons. They enjoyed it immensely and had great fun, everyone being friendly and nice.

On one particular afternoon, a few members who had attended the classes the longest were asked to chose three other people, to make groups of four. Lily a cheerful but tremendously obese person, who's whole body shook when she laughed, and wobbled when she walked, chose my mother, her friend Patsy and a tiny, elderly and shrivelled little woman called Tilley as her team.

The idea of this test was not only a bit of fun, it was also to see how they would react in an emergency, for their attentiveness to their patient, bandaging and general dealing with the situation.

'Here is your patient,' called their instructor, as a door opened and an elderly gentleman emerged. He followed the Instructor across the room and laid himself down on the chalk marks she had made on the wooden floorboards. He was dressed in a pair of dungarees, with a tattered shirt. His head, the sides of his face, an arm and a leg were covered in a red dye to simulate blood.

'You may pretend you are out for a walk,' smiled their instructor, 'when an enemy plane is heard to pass overhead. You hear the explosion as a bomb is dropped. It is close by, so as members of a first aid group you run to see if you can offer assistance should it be needed.'

'This gentleman's house has received a direct hit, but luckily he has been blown out through the window. Talk amongst yourselves for a few minutes to decide how you will deal with the situation and his injuries. When you are ready we will start with number one team, and that's yours Lily.'

'Oh my God', moaned Tilley, wringing her hands in dismay, 'my mind has gone blank already. I shan't be able to do anything correctly, I know I shan't.'
'Calm down do,' chuckled Lily her whole chest wobbling. 'Just follow me and do exactly as I do. The main thing is, to do our very best and get the most points. Are you all agreed?' Before they could answer the instructor said,
'When you are ready girls, you may begin.'

40

Lily glanced round at her little group, most of them on the verge of panic, at having to be the first to perform. Lily stuck up her thumb, winked and nodded confidently, then announced loudly, for the benefit of others in the room. 'Shall we go for a walk girls it's such a lovely day?' Lily then proceeded to walk, or as my mother said, waddle, around the room, gesturing with one hand, for the rest to follow. They did so, feeling very self-conscious, wondering if this was what their instructor had intended. Suddenly without warning she stopped. They all bumped into her.

When they had disentangled themselves, Lily put her hand to her ear, saying in her loud voice, 'Hark, I hear a Jerry plane, it's coming right over us, we'd better jump in this ditch for safety.'

With a leap that shook the whole room, Lily jumped sideways, instantly crouching down. There came a loud pop as she did so, like the cork from a champagne bottle, followed by a rending sound, in which my mother who was behind Lily saw the best part of the back of her skirt part company.

'Did you hear that girls?' called Lily quite unabashed. 'An explosion, must have been a bomb, the noise came from over there.' Lily pointed to the man laying on the floor. To everyone's surprise he lifted his head and said rather crossly,
'Oh no it didn't madam. You are not blaming me for that.' My mother said she felt so embarrassed; her face went the colour of a beetroot.

The rest of the gathering were in fits of laughter, but without batting an eyelid Lily carried on. 'Look girls, the bomb made a mess of that house, there is something laying over there. Why it's a poor injured man, just look at all that blood. What a blessing we have all been learning first aid so we can help him.' She dashed forward.

'Bandages Tilley please, find some bandages,' yelled Lily. As Tilley rushed off Lily knelt down beside the patient to assess the damage. 'The ankle is broken,' she declared after a while, 'with deep cuts to the leg caused by glass as he was blown out through the window. You two will deal with that,' she told my mother and her friend.

41

'I'll do the cuts to hand and arms, that will leave Tilley to deal with the face and head injuries.'

All was quiet as they set to work, until Tilley who was kneeling beside Lily suddenly shot back sharply, bumping into Lily who couldn't help knocking into Patsy, who cracked heads with my mother. The bandage in her hand was flung across the floor, unrolling as it went.

'What's wrong?' demanded Lily crossly. 'Tilley can't you manage those head injuries?

'Yes I can,' came the shocked reply. 'When I thought he was unconscious I could, but he isn't is he?' she stated indignantly. 'As I went to bandage his head he opened one eye and winked at me.'

'Take no notice Tilley, just carry on,' giggled Lily. 'The reason he did it is because he's got concussion, poor man. Bring the bandage down a bit to cover his eyes.' As my mother and Patsy finished what they had to do, they stood up. Lily remained kneeling until Tilley was also ready, then quickly she checked over their work. Satisfied at last she went to rise, her foot caught in her skirt, she toppled forward, right onto their patient.

With a grunt, clearly audible all over the room, the breadth was crushed from his body. For a few seconds nobody moved, it was if they were paralysed, then a bunch of watchers rushed forward. It took four of them to lift Lily to her feet. More attended to the patient, who was now a real patient. Laying on the floor, trussed up like a chicken, his feet bandaged together, arm in a sling, head and face covered in bandages.

Poor Lily was most upset, she wept, thinking at first that she had killed him. Fortunately he was only bruised and badly shaken but declined to act as their practicing patient anymore, saying he did not think he would survive if another two ton Tessie fell on him. My mother and her friend Patsy never went back to first aid classes. Although what happened was not their fault, they were just too embarrassed.

It was strange in the village now. All eligible husbands and sons had been called up, the only males left were elderly, or men unfit for service and young boys not yet old enough to join the forces. With no men to do the work. Women were having to take over their jobs; sometimes successfully, sometimes not quite as well.

Grandma took me with her when she went to visit relatives one day. It was a long. long way to walk. I was tired on arrival, Grandma said 'If we are to get home today, we'd best catch the bus.' When the time came, we walked almost a mile to the bus stop and waited there. When the bus appeared, we had grave doubts as to whether it was going to stop. It was travelling so fast. However it pulled up with a squeal of brakes several yards down the road. We had to run to get on.
'Hurry along there,' shouted the conductress, 'we haven't got all day.'

The bus started with a jerk. The driver also a woman and obviously quite unused to driving a bus it seemed. 'We are out to make a good impression.' We heard the conductress informing a customer, 'This is our first trip.'

Our corner stop soon came into view. We prepared to get off the bus as the bus slowed. Then to our surprise, instead of stopping, it turned off the normal bus route, travelling along the lane that would take us nearly home. Grandma giggled as the bus picked up speed, 'Save us having to walk so far,' she whispered.

The conductress was busy talking still, as our road fast approached, so grandma stood up and rang the bell. The brakes were applied instantly. The bus gave a shudder, poor grandma fell over backwards, onto the seat she had just vacated. The conductress sat down with a thump onto the lap of a gentleman nearby, her mouth hanging open with shock. The expression on her face so amused me. Childlike I giggled thinking she looked so funny.

Grandma staggered to her feet again, quickly hustling me off the bus. Looking back she called, ' I don't know if you are aware of the fact, but you left the usual bus route and are on the wrong road.' The conductress walked shakily down the aisle, glared balefully at us.

'Thank you for your kind information Madam,' she snarled, 'I don't need it. I know exactly where I am thank you very much. In future if you travel on my bus keep your hand off my bell.'
'Good luck to you then' shouted grandma as the bus moved off, 'and they'll need it,' she muttered. 'I don't think they will get far, maybe if we wait a few minutes we'll see.'
'See what?' I asked.
'You'll soon see,' she replied then realising what she had said we giggled.

I was getting impatient, wanting to be off home to tell my mother all about my day out, when we heard the bus returning. As it passed us, Grandma and I stood watching and waving till it was out of sight.

We heard later, the bus got stuck behind a horse and cart. The bus driver had tooted her horn loudly, impatiently and continuously, until fed up the angry man with the horse went back, asking the driver not very politely. 'What the hell she thought she was doing, with a damn great vehicle like that on a narrow road like this and pipping her horn, frightening his horse.' 'Clear off back where you came from,' he said. 'We never have buses come down this way and don't want them neither.' After consulting with the conductress they decided to turn the bus round in a field gateway and come back.

Fortunately this was an isolated occasion. Other jobs that women took over they did very well. They went round on bicycles delivering mail, land girls worked on the farms, milking cows, seeing to other farm animals and helping to get the harvest in. We children collected whatever was being collected. We gathered blackberries for the WRVS for jam making and rosehips from the hedgerows, for making rosehip syrup. The boys sometimes collected acorns for the farmer's pigs.

Chapter 4 Footprints in the snow.

One morning two silver specks appeared in the sky, they moved so slowly we watched them for ages wondering what they were. There was no sound, which made it more frightening. A friend called Charlie came by and suggested they were the new secret weapon old Hitler had sent over. He thought that when they got above us they would drop something and blow us out of existence.

We were relieved when they missed us and drifted out to sea. Sometime later two aeroplanes flew over and we heard gunfire. Rumour had it that the mysterious objects were barrage balloons that had drifted over, after having broken free from their moorings round one of the big towns. The planes had shot them down.

We were sitting with our neighbour one evening at her house, during the most terrible air raid, the worst there had been for several weeks. My sisters, both worn out, were fast asleep on the sofa for it was getting very late. My mother, Annie and me were wide awake, listening with bated breath to all the noise outside. Planes roaring overhead laden with bombs, continuous gunfire from along the coast, as they tried to shoot down the enemy planes as they flew in, the distant thud and bangs of exploding bombs. The sky, when my mother went to look was full of flashes from bombs, tracer and glows in the sky from fires. Searchlights reared up into the night sky, trying to pick out enemy aircraft so the guns could shoot at them.

Finally at about half past ten, long after our bed time, things began to quieten down. My mother decided now was the time to get us back home and into bed. We left my elder sister there as she was so sound asleep.

Back home Eliza asked for a drink, my mother went to the pantry to get her one, just as another German plane flew over. Mother dashed back into the room shrieking, 'Get under the table quick, something just whined past the pantry window and landed with a ghastly thump outside!'

We huddled in terror, expecting any second that a bomb would go off and the house would be blown apart, and us with it. My hands were pressed firmly over my ears so I wouldn't hear the bang when it came.

As time went by and nothing happened, we gradually began to relax. My mother kept muttering to herself, 'I didn't imagine it, I know I didn't, I distinctly heard the whining noise and that almighty thump, right outside the window, I know I did.'

Every few seconds she went to the door, listening for the all clear to sound, when it did she picked up her coat and said she was going outside to look around. 'No, no,' I pleaded with her, 'don't go. It's dark and dangerous out there. You won't be able to see.'

'If you stand on something, it might go off. Besides what you heard may have a delayed action fuse. It's probably sitting out there just waiting for you to go and trigger it off.'
'Don't you worry.' she replied quite confidently, 'I'll be very careful.'

Nothing I said would deter her. She just wouldn't be content until she had been, I knew, but I was so frightened for her safety. I didn't know what we would do if anything happened to my mother. I was most relieved when, after a few minutes, she returned. 'You were right,' she said, 'It is too dark to see, but that isn't to say there is nothing there.'

My younger sister, tired out had fallen asleep under the table, so grabbing a cushion I curled up beside her. My mother pulled the big armchair close and made herself comfortable in that and so we spent the night. At the crack of dawn, she was up and outside, energetically hunting around to try and find what had caused the mysterious thump she had heard.

Mother found nothing to account for it. A neighbour across the way was an early riser too. Mother decided to go across and inform him about what had happened. He came immediately to help her search. After hunting all around and finding absolutely nothing, he told her she must have been dreaming when she heard the thump, and this she firmly denied.

After breakfast our friends turned up, 'Are you coming to watch the fun?' they asked. 'We've been there for ages already. There is a lot of activity going on, soldiers, lorries and things. They say there is an unexploded bomb in the field. Everyone has been evacuated from the houses nearest to it, in the next road. We are going back to watch. There are loads of people there.'

We eyed my mother uncertainly. We didn't want to miss any of the excitement. After asking a few questions, she nodded, 'Alright off you go, behave yourselves and don't get in the soldiers' way.' We were off like a shot, just in case she changed her mind, running up the road and around the corner, to stand with groups of other people, old men women and children.

We couldn't see much for a couple of soldiers stood guard on the gate leading into the field. They allowed nobody to enter except army vehicles and more soldiers. An officer came across and explained to us about there being an unexploded bomb, in the far corner of the field. The soldiers were trying to dig it out to defuse it. Apparently they were having a few problems, for as they dug the bomb kept sinking deeper and deeper into the thick clay soil.

After that most of the adults went home, apart from two pensioners, who obviously hadn't seen each other for several months, by the way they were talking. Several vehicles came and went, strange looking vehicles with red painted mudguards, which one of the chaps said, belonged to the bomb disposal squad. He also said, 'When they get that there bomb out, they'll put it in one of them jeeps, then rush off, hell for leather with it to some waste ground and blow it up.'

I was listening to him taking it all in, when I suddenly turned round and saw my mother hurrying past. Mother went over to the soldiers at the gate. 'Could I have a word,' she said. 'I think that there may have been more than one bomb come down last night. During the air raid I distinctly heard a horrible whining noise, then a loud thump right outside my pantry window. I have hunted around but can't find anything.

I was close to the window when I heard it and I'm not one to make things up, so don't dismiss it as some old woman's ravings.'

The soldier laughed, 'No we won't do that Madam. If you heard something, then you heard something. Look hang on a second, I'll see if I can find someone to speak to you.' After about 10 minutes an officer appeared and mother retold her story.

'Only one bomb was reported dropped Madam.' He told her. 'But there could be another explanation for the thump you heard. These bombs have been known to hit the ground with such force that they bounce. I should think that's quite probably what happened in this case. Think yourself lucky it didn't explode last night, or you wouldn't be standing here talking to me now.'

My mother went away still unconvinced, she'd never heard of a bomb bouncing before and wondered if the soldier may have told her that to get rid of her. Back home she hunted round once more outside the window where she heard the thump, as before she found nothing, not even a dent in the ground.

The soldiers words came back to her, 'these bombs have been known to bounce.' 'Of course,' she muttered, feeling enlightened. 'If they bounce I've probably been looking in the wrong direction. It could have bounced right over the house and be somewhere at the top of our vegetable garden.'

Seconds later, she walked up the garden path at the front of the house, gazing in all directions. Suddenly she stopped dead in her tracks, 'I knew it,' she muttered triumphantly, 'I just knew it. There it is, I was right all along' Mother stared ahead at the very top of the garden where it was slightly over grown. Her eyes rested on a small patch of fresh earth, with something sticking out the top. 'I wasn't wrong, I knew I wasn't, there was another bomb.'

Mother turned and began to run back down the path, almost bumping into father. 'Don't go up there,' she screamed at him. 'There is an unexploded bomb. Stay here in case the children come back, and for heaven's sake, don't let them go near it, it might explode. I'll run round and report it to the soldiers.'
'Here wait a minute,' he grabbed her by the arm. 'Before you go running off, you'd best explain to me where it is, so I don't go and tread on it.'

'There,' she said pointing, 'You can just see it, where that little mound of earth is.'

He roared with laughter, 'Good God woman, that isn't a bomb, it's where I've just started digging a hole to empty the lavatory bucket in. That's the handle of my spade sticking up, go and look if you don't believe me!'

Father couldn't resist telling his mates the story. Soon it was all around the village. My poor mother was a long time living it down. For months afterwards people would ask, 'Have you found any bombs recently?' Mother maintained till the day she died, that one day another bomb would be found.

Round the corner in the field, the soldiers toiled, digging their way deeper and deeper after their elusive bomb. Towards evening, everyone was warned to stand well back and to leave the gate and the road clear because they had reached the bomb. After it had been defused, brought up to the surface and loaded onto one of their vehicles, they would need to make a quick exit from the field and away. Should the bomb explode during transit, some of us could be hurt or killed.

The few adults who had returned to watch went home again. We children retreated into a meadow, and watched from over the hedge, until my mother came looking for us and ordered us home. The few of our pals who remained said later that soon after we had gone a vehicle came tearing out of the gateway, roaring off up the road like an express train.

Rumour had it, that as the soldiers drove off with the bomb it started to tick, so it apparently had two fuses. They reached the nearest waste ground, unloaded the bomb and stood well back. When it exploded it was fortunate that nobody was hurt. Nearly the whole village went round later that evening, to view the hole the soldiers had dug. It was enormous, like looking down a well shaft and there right at the very bottom, so deep you could hardly see it, was the indentation of the bomb.

Great auntie was full of praise for those courageous young men, those dear brave boys who had dug out the bomb. 'Not for anything,' she said, 'would I have the nerve to be at the bottom of that great hole, with no escape should that thing have exploded.'

Like most people we had problems with our sugar ration. It just didn't go very far, especially as we all had a sweet tooth. We argued so much my mother divided our sugar into five jars with our names on. This was alright for a few days, then we noticed someone was helping themselves to our sugar. Mother admitted it was her. She had taken some out of each jar for cooking purposes. If we wanted sugar in cakes and puddings, we would have to lose some of our ration. Finally came the day when we ran out, so golden syrup was tried in cakes and buns with great success, then in stewed fruits and custards.

Condensed milk was another substitute for sugar. A tablespoonful stirred into your stewed apple was absolutely delicious, but like all tinned goods they cost you precious points and we only had so many per month.

One Christmas things were particularly bad. Our grocer shared out his allocation of dried fruit as best he could to all his customers. We had two ounces of sultanas, two ounces of currants, the very pippy ones that people said were dried elderberries, five prunes (one each) and half a packet of dried dates. Out of this my mother made mincemeat which was mostly apple, a Christmas pudding and a Christmas bun each. There wasn't enough to make a cake.

We had a tin of sausages. My mother considered them a good buy, although they took a lot of points. The fat inside the tin was used to make the pastry for a few sausage rolls and the crust of a sausage patty on Boxing Day. The day after, we had a sausage pudding, made from the scrapings of the sausage tin and a few remaining pieces of sausage. Even after that she had half a cup of fat for frying.

Our Christmas dinner? Well, father came home with a cock pheasant hidden under his coat, he said it had run out in front of his bike and he'd run over it. Rather than leave the poor thing laying there for somebody else to pick up, he'd brought it home. We were warned not to say anything, in case the police got to

50

hear and came to arrest father and put him into prison, so it was a very hush, hush affair.

There were no orange or bananas to put in our stockings. There were none in the shops, in fact, I couldn't remember what a banana tasted like. My mother had been shopping and bought one or two things for our stockings. My main present was a jigsaw of a British submarine. I did it over and over until I knew it by heart. It was hard work as it was not interlocking.

The local brickworks had now closed. One afternoon the owner came to the door to ask my father if he would be interested in keeping an eye on the place. (To be the caretaker) It was too far for him to come every day, but father lived close by.

Naturally father was delighted, as he couldn't go and fight for his country, he felt at least he would be doing something important. The owner also said, 'Don't let the rabbit population take over. Set a couple of snares now and again to keep them down. You can have the rabbits, I don't want them.' It was a sight to see father, two or three times a day strolling around the brickworks as though he owned the place.

He acquired a couple of snares from somewhere. Soon we had rabbit pie, rabbit stew, baked rabbit, you name it we had it. Finally the day came when my mother said 'Enough is enough, I'm not cooking another rabbit for a very long time,' so father had to give them away.

One winter's morning very early when it was overcast and barely light, there came a sudden bang on the door. It was so loud that it woke the entire household, we heard shouting too. Grumbling father got out of bed, went across to the window and pulled the curtain aside to peer out.

On the doorstep stood our neighbour from across the way, 'Sorry to disturb you this time of the morning mate,' he shouted. 'I've been so worried I hardly had a wink of sleep all night. About half past nine yesterday evening, we heard a knock on our door. When I opened it two strange men stood there, asked if I knew of anywhere they could spend the night.'

'They said they were on a walking holiday, I thought that sounded suspicious, I mean who would go on a walking holiday this weather, they were a bit rough and ready and talked like foreigners, I could hardly understand them. They had no luggage that I could see apart from one small black case.'

'I told them there was no body around here that took in lodgers. They'd best carry on down to the pub and enquire there. After I'd explained to them where to go they left and I went to bed. It was such a cold night, I couldn't sleep for thinking about them, wondering if they managed to find somewhere out of the bitter wind, it was enough to flay you alive.'

'It struck me they could have been a couple of German spies, or somebody up to no good. The wife said "Don't lay there thinking about it. Get up and go and look around," so I did. As you can see there has been a good fall of snow and if you're interested, two sets of footprints going up to your brickyard. I reckon those two must have spent the night in one of your sheds.'

Father gave a great big proud smile at the mention of his brickyard and his sheds. Suddenly he seemed wide awake, 'I'll be right with you.' he said abruptly. Never had I seen him move so fast. Of course I got up as well. I wanted to know exactly what was going on, besides hadn't his friend said there had been a fall of snow?

There was another reason too, since father had snapped my first bayonet in two, I had managed to fashion another stick, of which I was very proud, being much thicker and sharper than the previous one. It was as yet untried, but I was longing to get it out of hiding and use it on a German.

If those two men turned out to be spies, they were certainly going to feel the point of it, right where it would hurt them most. Of that I was determined. So I followed father up the path with it clutched firmly in my hand. We joined father's friend who was waiting impatiently for us behind the hedge near the road.

At father's inquiring look, he shook his head, 'Not seen hair nor hide of anyone,' he reported quietly. 'Alright' nodded father, striding importantly across the road to inspect the evidence. 'By gad, them two chaps have got big feet,' he muttered. 'Size eleven I reckon or maybe twelve. Now you and the gal had better stay here behind the hedge out of sight. If anyone comes down the yard, whatever you do, don't confront them you might get hurt. Just keep your eyes on them and watch where they go. I'll be back soon.'

'Yes Sergeant,' we both answered, clicking our heels together and saluting him. He glared at us for a second or two, then off he went, hurrying along in the direction of great auntie's house to return five minutes later carrying a rifle and a long pronged, dangerous looking pitchfork.

'This is your weapon. Don't be afraid to use it if you have to,' he instructed, handing the fork to his friend. 'I'll keep the rifle. Now you and I are going to take a walk up my brickyard and flush them buggers out. No not you gal,' he muttered crossly as I went to follow with my bayonet held ready to jab the Germans. So, disappointedly I had to stand back and watch as the two men set off.

Father led the way, the rifle pointed in front of him, he wore a long black scarf wound round and round his neck, the two ends hanging down below the bottom of his old army greycoat. He had mentioned his scarf had grown since he wore it last year, He didn't know why. We children did. Unable to find rope to make a swing under the apple tree during the summer, we had used his scarf and severely stretched it.

Behind him walked his friend, who seeing my disappointment turned to wave, making me laugh as he pretended to jab father with the fork. They stopped often to gaze around looking for anything suspicious.

I had now been joined by, my mother and sisters. While I was bringing them up to date on events, father's friend's wife turned up, followed by great auntie. Two of our school friends, out enjoying the snow, saw us all standing there and inquired as to what was going on, so there was quite a gathering.

Out of sight now, the two men continued to follow the trail of the mysterious footprints. They made slow progress, stopping occasionally so father could study the foot prints which he did with grim determination, how dared these strangers venture up into his brickyard without permission he thought, leaving a blazing trail of evidence behind them.

At the top of the track, it seemed the owners of the footprints had come to a halt, obviously hesitating a few seconds as if wondering which way to go. They carried on down one side of a long shed, where bricks were stored when they were drying out. Round the bottom they went and back up the other side, round another building and down both sides of another long shed. The two men crept stealthily along, wanting to surprise whoever was unofficially in residence somewhere along the way.

Finally after following the trail to almost every shed and building in the site father came to a sudden halt. He could see the footprints led straight to a small wooden shed set apart from all the rest. 'Aha' he grunted with satisfaction, 'so that's where the buggers have gone to roost. Hey you in there, the place is surrounded, we are all armed, so come out with your hands in the air.'

At that moment, his companion in trying to get a better view, slipped, accidentally jabbing father a rather forceful blow with the pitchfork. He leapt into the air, yelling with shock, his finger automatically tightening on the trigger.

The gun went off with aloud bang, echoing round the quiet countryside, pellets slammed into the door of the shed, which swung open with a ghostly creak, revealing the shed to be empty. Meanwhile, hearing the gun go off, we all stepped into the road, all anxiously scanning the track to the brickyard.

Another 10 minutes or so elapsed before two bedraggled figures appeared, both covered in snow. Great auntie was so relieved she ran to meet them, 'Thank God you are both safe. How proud we all are of two such brave men. What happened up there? did the spies try to evade capture so that you had to shoot them?'

'No', answered father, with a hasty glance at his companion, 'They were artful and got away over the fields at the back.' 'Got away?' I shouted angrily, 'you let them get away? They wouldn't have done if I'd been with you. It's not fair. You knew I wanted to use my bayonet.'

'Bloodthirsty little pest,' muttered my father, turning instantly to Auntie as she suggested the men went over to her house for a drop of her rhubarb or parsnip wine, to help them get over the shock. As they left the little gathering dispersed.

The story spread round the village. A couple of days later the local policeman came to the door wanting to know if there was any truth in the rumours of two German spies being seen in the village.

Father accompanied him over to the neighbour's house, who then had to admit it had all been a hoax. He was a real joker and had seen the opportunity to pull a fast one on father. Knowing how proud father was of his responsibility for caring for the brickyards, he had risen early, seen the snow that had fallen overnight and thought 'Now is my chance.'

Wearing Wellington boots, he had walked all the way up the track to the brickyard, then up and down the sides of the long sheds that housed the bricks until he reached the small shed set apart. Once he reached the door of that building, he walked all the way backwards, round the side of the sheds and down the track until he reached his starting point. The result, two sets of footprints going up. No wonder father was fooled.

He tried to make out he had known all along, but had gone along with it. We didn't think he really had otherwise why did he go and disturb great auntie and borrow the rifle and pitchfork? As for my sharpened stick, my bayonet. I put that away for another day, hoping that the time would eventually come, when I could poke a German with it and really make him run.

Chapter 5 Red Indians and the Soldiers.

We had a lot more snow over the next few days and a little bit of excitement. The horses pulling the snowplough got stuck and were floundering in snowdrifts that came up past the tops of their legs. They had to be dug out and the clearing of the lane was abandoned.

The main roads were blocked by huge drifts. As we struggled to school we saw soldiers with shovels who were trying to clear them.. They piled snow like walls on both sides of the road. Worst of all, the allocation of coal to the school hadn't arrived.

The teachers warned us the supply was very limited. From now on the fires would not be made up after one 'clock, in order to preserve the remaining coal. If we would like to bring a spare coat or woolly to school, we could sit in class with it on, to help keep us warm. They also said, 'If you have any spare logs at home, or find any wood on your way to school, could you please bring it along to help eke out the coal.'

No logs arrived. No family could spare any. We were all in the same boat, everyone being short of fuel, and having problems to keep warm. A rumour went round the school, that when we ran out of coal the school would have to close and we'd have a holiday. That suited us just fine.

However the teachers heard this rumour and told us that contrary to what we might think, the school would not close. Even if we ran out of coal completely, we would still have to go as usual and sit in class with our hats, coats, scarves and mittens on. Well if that was the case, we thought, we might as well see if we could find some wood.

On our way to school next morning we made a start by searching both sides of the hedgerow that bordered the road, breaking off all the thick old stumps, and it was surprising how many we found. Soon we had piles laying all the way along the road.

Collecting it all into one heap posed a big problem, but worse was to follow. It now had to be transported to school. There was too much to carry a few pieces each. In the end we dragged and carried it from one heap to the next. Gradually getting closer and closer to the school.

How thrilled we were when we laid our first tiny heap in the middle of the playground, then raced back down the road for more and more. Finally it was all there. We stood around surveying our efforts proudly. In spite of the snow underfoot, we were as warm as toast, our faces red and glowing and perspiring freely. All filled with the satisfaction of a job well done.

'We'd better go into school now and tell the teacher,' said one lad, 'I bet she'll be ever so pleased with us.' We entered the cloakroom and hung up our coats and hats, then the five of us stood near the door and gently knocked.

We had to knock several times before the door was opened. The teacher stood glaring at us, 'I have been expecting you' she said grimly. 'Come along in, stand in a row in front of me if you please.' We didn't like the sound of that but did as we were told.

'School,' she said picking up her ruler and running it through her hands, 'starts at nine o'clock in the morning in case you have forgotten, not ten fifteen.'
A hand shot up in the air, 'Please Miss, you said we were short of coal and needed wood for the fires so we collected some. Just you look out in the playground, there is a lovely big pile out there.'

'I have no wish to go and look in the playground, child, thank you very much,' she snapped. 'What concerns me is, you are late for school. I waited till ten o'clock before marking you all absent. Now, before going to your places hold out your hands.'

That ruler descended twice on each of our hands, once on the front and once on the back, making us feel hurt, bewildered and resentful. All our energy, our hearts and souls had gone in collecting that wood to keep as we thought the school fires burning a little longer.

For all our efforts we had been rewarded with punishment. She was right of course. We shouldn't have been collecting wood when we ought to have been in school, but we had been so busy, the time had passed quickly and we hadn't realised it was so late. Life just did not seem fair.

At playtime the other children stood round our woodpile, admiring and marvelling at the amount of wood we five had managed to drag to school. The two teachers said not a word. When we told our parents what had happened, they said we should have dragged the wood homeward. It would have been more appreciated. All week our wood remained in the playground, but on Monday it had gone. Near the school buildings sat a neat pile of logs all ready for the fires, sawn and chopped into lengths by good hearted villagers living nearby.

Lessons had just started, when a lorry bringing our allocation of coal arrived, so our wood wasn't needed after all, yet gradually we noticed the heap got smaller. It was mystifying. Where was our wood going we asked each other. Then someone said they had seen the teachers cycle past, with their bicycle baskets full of wood. So we kept watch and, sure enough, they loaded their baskets up every night until it was all gone.

A new mantel was needed for our Aladdin Oil lamp. The present one was frail with use and age and had a hole in one side. We thought also that a few cups and saucers might come in handy. Therefore my mother, Eliza and I, my mother's friend and her daughter (who was the same age as me) all set out on a trip to Southwold the nearest town.

We walked all the way as we usually did. It was only about four and a half miles, then of course we had the same journey back. People were poor in those days and bus fares cost money. The hardware shop was our first port of call. They had neither cups and saucers nor mantel for the lamp. They were very hard to come by, as due to the war very few were made.

There was the possibility some might come in the following week. Mother's name was added to a list of about twenty others. Now it was up the street to the fish shop. We were lucky here and when the grownups had bought what they wanted, we children clamoured for a peep at the sea.

The beach was mined in case the Germans tried to invade. Great rolls and coils of barbed wire were everywhere. Soldiers stood on guard around the guns and we passed many walking along the road. The sea was so calm and a beautiful blue, we would have been happy to stand there all day just looking at it.

Our parents however wanted to be getting out of town. There was always the possibility of an air raid, so back down the street we walked. Then what they feared might happen did. The siren went. We had never been so close to it before, it sounded horrific, absolutely blood curling.

My mother stopped dead, 'Oh my God,' she cried, 'What do we do now?' shops were closing. People in the street seemed to have vanished. One second they were all there and the next they had all gone.

'We'd better hurry and get out of town,' declared Patsy, 'Before them Jerries start dropping bombs.' 'Yes come on, lets run,' said my mother, clasping my sister's hand and leading the way. I and Patsy's daughter went next, leaving Patsy to bring up the rear. An aeroplane came in low over the sea, the guns began firing making a dreadful racket. Suddenly my mother swerved and ran into someone's gateway.

A tree stood in the middle of a small lawn and it was to this my mother headed. Finally gasping she huddled down beneath it. 'This will give us a little protection', she gasped as we all joined her. As the plane roared overhead, we felt so grateful for the shelter, then a movement at the window of the house caught our eyes. Staring out at us were three children, two elderly adults and a large shaggy dog. The children were laughing and pointing.

We felt so embarrassed as we looked at each other, then without a word up got my mother running out of the gateway and on down the road. Puffing and panting one behind the other we followed. We managed to get nearly out of town when the guns began again, another aircraft was heard roaring over low. Caught out in the open my mother shouted, 'Quick get down, get down!' We dropped to the ground immediately, folding our arms over the backs of our necks as we had been taught at school.

Patsy was the last to drop. She was a rather stocky well built woman and went down with a thump, landing on the edge of her shopping bag. Her fish, wrapped only in a single sheet of newspaper, shot out of her bag, travelling a little way up the road, where it slid alongside my mothers face. Feeling the cold wet scaly thing, she emitted a blood curling scream. You'd thought she was being murdered.

Our first thought was, she had been hit by something dropped from the plane. Then of course mother realised what the object was and began to laugh. Alerted by her screams, a dear old gentleman, his spectacles perched on the end of his nose, peered cautiously over the fence. A look of amazement crossed his face, 'What are you lot a doing, laying down there, gitting your clobber all mucky?' he asked.

As the others were still sitting there doubled with laughter, I seemed to be the only one capable of speech. 'We heard the siren go, then the guns firing at a plane that was coming over low, we thought it might fire at us,' I replied.
He tutted loudly, 'all that blooming row, I thought you had escaped from a mad house. Why you silly lot of fools, that plane wouldn't have hurt you.' He spoke in a disgusted tone of voice, 'That be one of ours.'

After that, whenever my mother or her friend had need to go into town, they went on their bikes, if they were in working order, or if not they borrowed one, or each others, then got out of town as fast as they could pedal.

My elder sister, now the proud owner of a new bicycle, given to those children who lived more than three miles away from the senior school, had taken to going on cycle rides with her friend. One day greatly daring, they rode into town to have a look at the damage done the night before during an air raid. Pushing their bikes they walked along looking in amazement at the huge piles of rubble, that the previous day had been houses with people living in them.

Suddenly from beneath one pile, they heard what they thought was the faint whimpering of a dog. They listened again, then spoke to soldiers who were passing. They quickly moved into action and a small dog was dug out. My mother was furious when she heard where they had been, but when she calmed down said, 'They must have been meant to go, but to stay away in future as it is too dangerous.'

Dreadful happenings were heard of every day. Eavesdropping on my grandfather and his friend, I overheard more than I had bargained for. 'We had a rum old job this week,' said the friend. 'Remember hearing about those two idiots that wandered down to the beach and got blown up? Well we had to go down and help remove them. One had the lower part of his body blown away, the other, oh dear me, apart from one arm, we had to literally scrape the rest of him up with a shovel.' Needless to say I had nightmares that night.

A gruesome story indeed but every day dreadful things were happening up and down the country. Rumour had it that further down the coast at a place called Shingle Street experimental and hush, hush things took place. One experiment had gone horribly wrong. Our chaps (some said) were approaching from the sea, pretending to be Germans, to test a new underwater device. It ignited killing and burning our own men.

When meeting with friends, relatives or neighbours, the main topic of conversation was usually the war. Someone always knew of somebody who's friends or relatives had just been killed, or badly hurt, perhaps buried under tons of rubble, hit by shrapnel or falling aircraft parts. Others were killed whilst on active service. There was no end to the terrible tales of disaster.

Occasionally we would hear of bodies being washed up on the beach. After being in the water several days they were often in pretty bad shape. According to the older boys at school who took great delight in teasing me, they said they were full of shrimps. I went home to ask my father if this was true, he chuckled and replied 'Yes I suppose so, shrimps are natural scavengers.' When I realised what he meant, I was physically sick, it put me off eating shrimps for life.

A neighbour spoke of a distant friend who came home on leave from the Navy, only to discover he had no home to go to. No family, no nothing. His house had received a direct hit by a bomb two weeks previously. His wife was holding a small birthday party for one of his three children. His mother, father and two aunts, all the family he had in the world, all were killed. The telegram informing him of this terrible tragedy had not caught up with him.

Hearing a rumour that the local gamekeeper was going to be out for the day, I and my friend Alex thought to seize the opportunity and creep into the nearby woods to play Red Indians.

Faces daubed with my mother's whitewash and my sister's lipstick, we looked a fearsome sight, or thought we did. Alex had a homemade bow and arrow. Not to be outdone I carried my father's small axe for a tomahawk. It was adorned with long strands of red and blue material and fitted into a piece of string, tied round my waist.

We were enjoying ourselves, being on the trail as we called it, creeping round in the middle of the wood, looking for signs of our imaginary enemies. When suddenly we heard what sounded like the roar of several approaching heavy vehicles, making their way along the narrow lane. Whatever could it be, we puzzled. Neither our neighbour's van nor father's friend's motorbike and sidecar sounded like that. This was something quite unusual.

Instead of going straight on past the wood, it sounded now as if they were pulling in and coming along the track. Then gradually one by one they stopped and we heard voices.

I glanced at my friend and found him eyeing me questioningly. We both felt scared. Instinctively we wanted to run away as fast as possible, yet we hung back, curious to know what other interlopers were trespassing in the wood.

'Quick,' he pulled my arm, 'let's shin up a tree out of sight, then we can look down and see what's going on.' Soon we were sitting astride a branch, fairly high up in the bushiest tree we could find, leaning back comfortably against the trunk. There was only disappointment, now we were up here. We could not see a thing and we dare not come down again, for the voices sounded closer.

It was fifteen to twenty minutes later when Alex gently touched my shoulder, his fingers held to his lips for silence. He pointed downwards. I peered through the foliage but could see nothing. Then I realised the small bushes in the glade below, seemed to have moved position, Alex leaned over and whispered in my ear, 'Soldiers in camouflage, must be on manoeuvres.'

We sat for ages after the 'bushes' had disappeared, but nothing else happened. Everywhere was silent. No birds sang, just a cock pheasant calling plaintively from the field beyond the wood. I soon got fed up sitting on the hard knobbly branch, with nothing to do or see. Finally I pulled out my tomahawk, I looked at it as I held it in my hands, then carefully whirled it round and round thinking how I would like to throw it at that old tree stump in the centre of the glade below. I practised aiming it again and again, my fingers itching to let it go.

Suddenly Alex who had been gazing down below, became aware of what I was doing. Thinking I was about to throw it, he flung out a hand to stop me. I was so startled, I relaxed my grip and the tomahawk sped on its way. It struck the target fair and square. I heard a muffled yell and stared open mouthed as the stump collapsed into a heap on the ground and a khaki clad figure wriggled free with a groan, to lay rubbing the upper part of his thigh.

Another soldier materialised as if from nowhere and moved to his side. Bending down he picked up my tomahawk. We distinctly heard the astonished words,
'Bloo---dy Hell.' He straightened up immediately, looking carefully all around him. 'If I didn't know better I'd say we were in the outback of America, and this dangerous looking weapon belonged to a young Red Indian brave on the warpath. You don't know what or who is hidden in this undergrowth.'

He helped the other soldier rise to his feet, retaining an arm round him. He helped him out of sight, taking my beloved tomahawk with him. The seriousness of the situation now struck me. 'What am I going to do now?' I moaned anxiously in my friend's ear. 'My father will half kill me if I go home without his axe.'

I got no sympathy, 'You should have thought about that before you started playing about with it,' he muttered angrily. 'As far as I can see, you've got two choices: one, get down the tree, find the soldiers and ask for it back. Mind you, you'll probably get us both into trouble, for being here in the wood and injuring that soldier. Or, you can go home and pretend to your father, that you never had his axe and don't know where it is.'

'He don't know I took it anyway,' I sniffed, I felt like bursting into tears, but not in front of Alex. That wouldn't do. I was supposed to be a brave Red Indian Chief, not a sissy. He appeared so angry with me. I didn't dare say anything more. We sat in silence for an eternity, neither seeing nor hearing another thing.

Anyway, I had no heart in our great adventure now, I was too busy worrying about my tomahawk and what father would say when he found it missing. In fact I was quite relieved when Alex poked me in the ribs and whispered. 'Time we were, off Red Bird.' I nodded miserably. We had a good look round beneath us then quietly slithered down the trunk of the tree.

As we neared the bottom and were about to slip away, a harsh voice shouted, ' Hands up!' I was so startled. I gave a shriek of alarm, my hands shooting up instantly. 'Don't try anything,' continued the voice, 'My gun is loaded, I shoot first, ask questions afterwards.' A soldier stepped into view from the undergrowth, lowering his gun he gazed at us in amazement, 'Crikey a couple of bloody kids.' 'What the hell are you doing here?'
I replied haughtily 'We are out on the trail,' then thought, ignorant palefaces like him, wouldn't know what 'on the trail' meant. After eyeing me up and down, he ignored me and turned his attention to Alex.
'Right kid, a straight answer please, how the hell did you come to be here in the wood?'
'By horse of course,' said Alex who was a bit of a wit, 'They are tied up over there. The chestnut belongs to Grey Wolf, that's me,

the grey belongs to Red Bird.' The soldier hesitated for a second, then grinned.

'I'm not falling for that one lad, I wasn't born yesterday, you haven't got any horses. So Grey Bird and Red Wolf, or whatever your names are, I think you'd better accompany me.'

Although we protested, we had no choice. He grasped each of us by the shoulder, hurrying us off through the bushes, until we came to the track that led into the wood. There hidden away amongst the trees and undergrowth, were three big lorries and a Bren gun carrier. There were two more further over. No wonder there had been an awful amount of noise.

A small group of soldiers stood talking together. One who looked like an officer, was holding my tomahawk in his hands. Marching us over to them, our captor released his hold and saluted. 'Found these two sir, climbing down a tree and about to slip off.'
Everyone was silent as the officer surveyed us from top to toe.
'Name?' he barked in a deep gruff voice, pointing at me,
'I Chief Red Bird,' I mumbled nervously.
'You?' he pointed at Alex.
'Chief Grey Wolf,' came his reply.
'You do realise,' snapped the officer, 'That you have delayed my manoeuvres, injured one of my men, as well as being in this wood, where you have no permission to be. Are you enemy agents?' I felt shocked that he should even think such a thing, while Alex spluttered indignantly. Pushing his shoulders back and standing up straight, he looked the officer in the eye and said firmly,
'No sir, we are not enemy agents, we are British through and through.'
'You,' he pointed at me again, 'Have you got anything to add to that?' his face was so stern and strict, it was frightening.
'I am not a spy sir,' I replied quietly.
'Good,' he sounded relieved, 'That solves one problem, doesn't it Corporal?, it saves having to shoot them at dawn.' My face paled further under my war paint,
'You wouldn't do that sir would you, not shoot us would you?'
'Most certainly,' was his reply, as if it was something he did every day of the week. 'If you were enemy agents spying on my manoeuvres, I wouldn't think twice about it.

Do you realise how dangerous it is for you in the wood, with all this going on. You could have been hurt, even killed. Nobody expected two Red Indians to be on the rampage in the middle of our battleground.'

He sounded impatient now as he said, 'Oh for goodness sake Corporal, take them home out of harms way. Take the jeep man and hurry.'

'Please,' I said eyeing the axe in his hands, my voice barely audible, 'May I have my tomahawk back?'

'Tomahawk?' he looked puzzled. 'Oh you mean this dangerous looking weapon? hardly the sort of thing for a little squaw to carry around is it?'

'I not a squaw!' I shouted indignantly, 'I Chief Red Bird of the Blackfeet Tribe.'

He stared at me with interest. 'The Blackfeet Tribe hey?'

'Yes' I snapped aggressively, fed up with him thinking I was just a lowly squaw. 'The Blackfeet Tribe, least that's what my father says when I take my shoes off.' He pushed the axe into my hands and turned quickly away.

The Corporal with a big grin on his face, put his big hand on my shoulder, 'Come on little Crabtree, this way.' Suddenly from behind came a great gust of laughter, the Corporal paused, 'And I thought he was angry,' he muttered.

He led us to a jeep that was almost hidden from sight beneath a pile of cut branches. He began pulling these off. 'Look,' said Alex, 'We don't want you to go to all this trouble, we can soon run home, it isn't far.'

'Wait,' snapped the soldier as we began to walk away, 'you both heard what the officer said. In case you've forgotten, I'll remind you. He said, take them home Corporal, use the Jeep and hurry. Now when a soldier is given an order, he has to obey. So in you get Bramblebush and you little Crabtree.' We were glad afterwards that we had, for to be driven home in style was so enjoyable, we told our driver we lived farther round the road than we did, so we had a longer ride. We dare not say anything to our parents about our great adventure or they would have skinned us alive.

Chapter 6
The Ship, the Strange Plane and the Invasion.

'Have you heard about the ship?' mother's friend opened our door and shouted excitedly. 'It was bombed and set on fire by a Jerry Plane. The crew thinking it was going to sink, abandoned it. Unmanned as it was, it drifted in with the tide and came ashore a few miles around the coast at Covehithe. The fire went out. They say if it is not too badly damaged, they are going to try to re-float her; tow her off by tug into deep water, as soon as the tide is right.'

'Lot's of people tell me they have been to look at the ship. It's a sight well worth seeing. I thought I would go tomorrow, do you fancy coming with me? It would be advisable not to leave it any longer, or it might be gone.'

As we hadn't heard anything about the ship, my mother wanted to know all the details, which her friend was eager to impart. After talking it over, they decided to go early the next morning. That would give them a chance to get back at a reasonably good time.

As it was such a long way to go, they would have to take their bicycles, my younger sister sitting on the back of my mother's bike. There was no way I could go with them, unless I ran all the way. I did offer but they would not agree to that.

I watched them pack their sandwiches and a bottle of drink next morning, trying not to appear envious. I even waved them off with a smile on my face, then went back indoors and ate the sandwiches that had been left for my lunch. Feeling peckish later I pinched one of father's. He'd gone off somewhere so wasn't there to see me.

He turned up at lunchtime, looked at his plate and eyed me suspiciously, muttering something about, not being enough to keep a sparrow alive. I took it to mean his sandwiches. He only had two left by that time. After eating them he glanced at the newspaper and went off again. The morning had seemed long, all on my own, but the afternoon was even longer.

My mother hadn't said what time she'd be back. I kept looking at the clock and lost count of the times I had gone outside to see if they were coming yet. By four o'clock I was getting really worried. I'll give them another half hour, I thought, if they are not in sight by then, I'm running over to grandma's house, to see if she has any idea where they could have got to.

My mind ran on. Could there have been an air raid and I hadn't heard the siren? A German plane could have flown over, seeing all the people standing near the beach looking at the ship and machine gunned them. Or, seeing the ship was ashore and in trouble, dropped another bomb on it and hit some of the watching people. I hadn't heard any explosions, but I wouldn't have done if the ship was as far away as my mother said.

All these things raced through my mind. At a quarter past four there was still no sign of them. I decided to stick to my plan and wait until half past before going over to grandma's. In the meantime I'd get my coat on ready. Taking one last look at the clock I strode determinedly out of the door. As I began to walk up the long path, somebody turned in from the road and began to walk towards me.

It was my mother. As she approached I noticed she was pushing the bicycle with one hand, my younger sister standing on the pedals, which was unusual. She normally sat on the carrier at the back. They stopped for her to get off, just as I caught up with them. Gaping in astonishment I noticed my mother balancing a huge lump of coal on the bicycle seat. It looked enormous. Never had I seen such a lump.

On the carrier at the back was another huge lump, tied in position by the belt from my mother's dress. That wasn't all. The tiny homemade bag she had taken their sandwiches in was stuffed with coal and stretched to nearly twice its original size. The handle, also stretched by the weight, allowed the bag to hang just above the ground. Mother's coat pockets bulged with coal.

Even her woolly hat, now clasped in my sister's hand, had a lump of coal in it.

I was so stunned. I said the first thing that came to mind, 'Did you see the ship?' 'Yes we did,' my mother replied. 'It nearly broke my heart, it's right up on the beach. Its cargo of coal is being unloaded so they can try and float her off. Coal lay on the beach and people were after it with sacks, old prams and wheelbarrows, even a little pony and trap.'

'Had I the means of getting it home, I could have had enough to last us right through the winter. I walked all the way home with this lot and if I wasn't so tired, I'd take some bags and go fetch some more. Take the bag off the handlebars, so I can wheel the bike round to the old shed and dispose of these two large lumps.'

As she eased the bag handle along I reached out with both hands to take it. It was so heavy I couldn't hold it. The bag landed on my big toe. If anyone was listening I am sure they would have heard my yell, right back at the ship where they were unloading the coal.

Over the next two or three days all I heard at school was about the ship. Everyone seemed to have been to see it except me. I began to feel more and more envious. Some children had even been and stood and watched as they tried to tow it off. It had been a failure, now they were waiting for a certain tide before trying again.

Father went out on Sunday morning and came rushing back as pleased as Punch. Someone had offered him a lift in their van to see the ship. Much to my father's disapproval my mother immediately went and asked if I could go too. The answer was yes. I could hardly contain myself. I was so excited. Before I departed, I was handed a large bag, 'Fill it up with coal,' said my mother. 'I'm sure they won't mind bringing it home in the van.'

I enjoyed my ride, which was quite a novelty for me. We arrived and parked the van and I danced with joy as we walked down to the beach. At last I was going to see the ship I had heard so much about.

There she was. I stood up and gaped. Never had I seen such a sight before. The deck was damaged and blackened by fire, there were patches of rust everywhere and she was firmly embedded in the sand. I ran across to get a better look. She was so big it was like looking up at the side of a mountain. I'd never seen a ship this close before. It was a long time before I could look away.

Then I realized I was still holding the bag and looked round for some coal. I searched and searched but could not find one piece, not the tiniest little bit. My mother was disappointed when I got home, 'What, no coal?' she said, 'Well never mind, at least you got to see the ship.'

We awoke one morning to the sound of an unusual aircraft. Priding ourselves we now knew the sound of every plane that flew over, be it British, American or German, this one had us all flummoxed. It was indeed a stranger.

Dressing hurriedly, we dashed downstairs and straight outside. There, flying round and round along the bottom of our garden, over our neighbour's garden and halfway down a field and back again, went this tiny, peculiar little plane.

Our whole family now stood on our garden path watching raptly. Then a neighbour arrived, some of our school friends who lived nearby, then a woman from down the road, all standing, gazing in wonder.

'What is it?' a voice asked,

'I don't know.' replied another. 'Might be something to do with old Hitler. He's up to all sorts of tricks, the old bugger. It's got no markings of any description that I can see. I don't recognise it as one of ours. Better not get too close to it.'

'Here comes Mr Marsh, he'll know,' said mother. We all looked round expectantly as another neighbour arrived.

'I see you're are all watching the Autogiro,' he greeted us. So now we knew what it was, we had heard about them but never seen one before. What was it doing flying about the bottom of our garden? That was the question no one seemed able to answer.

We went off to school and thought no more about it, but upon arriving home again we were amazed to see it still flying round. According to my mother it had been there most of the day. It departed in the early evening but next morning was back again flying round in the same monotonous circle.

During the next day or so news of the Autogiro spread through the village and many people walked down the long path to our house, asking if they might stand on our path for a few minutes to get a better view of the mysterious Autogiro.

Day after day and into the weekend, the tedious drone of the Autogiro began to irritate us. We stood beneath it as it flew over, making menacing gestures at it and shouting, but that brought no response. On Sunday afternoon Mr Marsh brought his friend, Mr Ben, who lived at the other end of the village and was supposed to know something about aircraft. He hoped he would be able to throw some light on the extraordinary behaviour of our unwanted visitor.

Mr Ben had brought his binoculars with him, but according to the two men as they stood talking, they thought it illegal to use them to look at a plane in wartime. They were afraid that if they were caught, they might have to answer questions from the police, or face interrogation from other investigators, to determine whether they were German spies or not. But as Mr Ben said, 'What the eye don't see, the heart don't grieve for.'

When the autogiro had flown past towards the other side of the circle, the two men laughing and giggling, raced across our neighbour's garden and quickly shinned up a large pear tree, hiding amongst the branches out of sight. Taking turns to study the autogiro as it went round. 'Acting like a pair of schoolboys,' muttered my mother.

Grandma now joined us. Mother was busy telling her about the two men up the pear tree with the binoculars, when we heard an almighty crack. The branch had snapped clean off the pear tree. As if in slow motion it descended. Now we could see the two men clinging on for dear life. They landed in a big clump of stinging nettles.

We roared with laughter at the funny sight. We just couldn't help ourselves. 'Talk about the daring young men on the flying trapeze,' chortled grandma, 'more like the daring men on the flying pear branch.'

We waited and watched, but when neither emerged after several minutes, my mother and grandma looked anxious. Mother said, 'We'd best run across, in case they need some help.' They found both men laying in the nettles, shocked, bruised and apparently groaning in agony. Mr Marsh was clutching at his bottom, in between groans he muttered that his spine was shattered, he had slammed his tail bone down on the thick end of the branch as he had landed.

Poor Mr Ben fared no better. He was clutching at his front with both hands. Both his feet had been jammed under the branch as they landed. Unfortunately for him, he had twisted his legs around the branch to keep his balance, while using both hands to hold the binoculars, and a huge knot in the wood had caught him such a thump in a very, very sensitive area.

I was quickly despatched indoors for two chairs for the gentlemen to sit on, but when I rushed out with them both men shook their heads, 'Oh, no, no, no' they couldn't sit down it was too painful. My mother after muttering a word or two to grandma, went off in the direction of Mr Marsh's house to confer with his wife. Mother returned several minutes later pushing his big wooden wheelbarrow stuffed with cushions.

With the two ladies' help he was soon laying face down across the wheelbarrow. Then with great effort and frequent stops my mother pushed him home. 'One down and one to go' mumbled grandma, a note of satisfaction in her voice. Then with a glance at Mr Ben, she left us saying, 'You stay here. Tell your mother if she returns before me that I won't be gone very long.'

It was indeed a relief to me when I saw my mother returning, for old Mr Ben hadn't said a word to me and I didn't know what to say to him. All he did was grip the back of one of the chairs I had brought out, sway backwards and forwards making little moaning noises, every now and again, which frightened me. Childlike I thought he was going to drop dead at my feet any second.

He refused the cup of tea my mother offered to make him and a glass of water to drink. He seemed angry she had asked him. He was too wrapped up in his pain and misery to be polite. We were all relieved and surprised, when after about 15 minutes grandma returned, pushing a man's bicycle with a rattly old trailer attached to the back. Inside lay one or two old coats and a couple of cushions.

Now their patient had to be persuaded to unclench his hands from the back of the chair. With many protests, moans, groans, oh's and ar's, he was installed inside the trailer laying flat on his back with his knees drawn up. This was the most comfortable position he could manage. Grandma said that was good, otherwise his feet would have hung out the back and we would have needed a bit of red rag to tie to them.

Soon the little cavalcade set off, grandma pushing the bike with the trailer attached to the back. Mother walked behind so she could keep an eye on their patient, at the same time, pushing his bicycle and carrying the binoculars. To my sister and I who had been left behind, they seemed to be gone forever. They had had to go three miles, explain to Mrs Ben what had happened, and get Mr Ben indoors. They were much quicker coming home they said because mother rode the bike and grandma sat in the trailer.

Whilst this was going on the Autogiro had continued to fly and did so for another couple of days. Then one morning it was no longer there. It did not return and was never seen again. Although one afternoon a Lysanda turned up and flew round and round on the same course as the Autogiro had.

The main difference was that each time he circled around he looked as if he was preparing to land in the corner of the field. This was done several times then the Lysanda flew off. We saw it pass overhead in the coming weeks but never again did it practise whatever it was doing at the end of our garden. We have learned since, that Autogiro's were used in the early forms of radar.

'It's a pitch dark night,' remarked my father as he peered out of the door. 'You can hardly see an inch in front of your nose. It's tidely rough too for the wind.' The wind gusted around us, not far off gale force and the rain lashed down but that did not deter father from leaving for an evening playing cards with his mates.

My mother with a coat flung over her head and shoulders, struggled out to the shed for some coal. On the way back she paused to listen, thinking she heard church bells ringing in the distance. Instantly on the alert, she listened hard and heard it again and yet again, that faint sound on the wind. Mother came in doors feeling extremely worried, for to hear church bells in wartime signified an invasion by enemy troops.

There had been no sound of planes flying overhead, I should think it's too bad a night for paratroopers to be dropped, she thought. If the Germans really have arrived, they must have taken advantage of the bad weather and crept across the sea by boat. No doubt they have come ashore along the coast and even now are making their way inland.

Several times after that she went to stand outside to listen, but heard nothing more than the wind howling round and rain still falling heavily. Surely, she thought, if it had been church bells I heard, other people would have heard them besides me? Or someone would have come and alerted us? The news would have travelled like wildfire, especially something as serious and important as this.

Unless of course, then the doubts set in, the German force is too big and strong and has overcome everything in its path. People have had no chance to notify others. Yet somebody had known, for the church bells have been rung.

Finally she sat down, but with the threat of impending invasion uppermost on her mind, she couldn't relax, being nervy and on edge the whole time. However the evening progressed rapidly and soon the time came for us to think about getting ready for bed. The kettle had boiled, the cups were out, my mother lifted the kettle to make the cocoa, when we heard footsteps go past our window.

We all looked up inquiringly, my mother had frozen, turning her head now to listen, still grasping the kettle in her hand. More

74

footsteps went past, sounding like a whole crowd of people. We heard a cough, then another from a little further along. Someone cleared their throat loudly.

Abruptly mother sprang to life, the kettle was returned swiftly to the top of the stove. She bent to pick up the heavy poker from the hearth waving it threateningly. 'My God,' she murmured, 'The German troops have arrived. I knew it was church bells I heard.'

Everywhere was in darkness as she swiftly turned out the oil lamp. Crossing to the window, mother carefully pulled aside the blackout curtains. It was too dark to see anything though we could still hear movement outside. Finally dropping the curtain back into place, she straightened up, while us children huddled together, frightened and miserable, at the sound of more footsteps tramping past.

Hardly daring to breathe, we listened for what seemed an age. At times it appeared as if dozens of people were milling around in our garden. 'This is all very suspicious,' whispered my mother, after an anxious fifteen minutes or so. 'I simply cannot understand why whoever is out there doesn't come to the door and make themselves known. They must realise that we can hear them.'

We flinched, tensing up as something brushed against the door, was it a hand fumbling for the door handle, so they could open it and come in? Our hearts thudded painfully We shook with fear. Mother hastily stepped forwards, poker held ready, but nothing happened, after a few seconds the footsteps moved away.

'I know,' I whispered suddenly, 'I've had a brilliant idea, 'Why don't I slip upstairs and look out of the bedroom window. Perhaps I can see who is out there.' I expected arguments, but to my surprise mother agreed instantly.

'Alright then, but you be very careful as you go up those stairs in the dark. We have enough to worry about here, without you falling down and hurting yourself. Another thing, whatever you do don't open or knock against the window, because who ever is out there, might think you're trying to attract their attention. Until we know who it is we don't want that to happen. Most importantly, should you hear this door burst open and strange men's voices, hide yourself up immediately under the bed and remain there, without making a sound, no matter what you hear going on down here.'

Off I went feeling so important as I crept up the stairs slowly, feeling my way in the darkness and wondering what on earth my mother meant by her warning. What was likely to happen if strange men came into the house. I had no idea.

The stairs door had been closed quietly behind me. Now I was on my own, alone in the darkness that closed around me like a shroud. Having negotiated the stairs safely, it took a few seconds to get my bearings, then I crept across the floor on hands and knees.

The curtains had been drawn across the window earlier. I now took hold of a corner and pulled it to one side, so I could peer out. There was movement in plenty both below and on the garden, but I could not see a thing. Never very brave in the dark, I sat my vigil as long as I dared, but it became increasingly scary up here, all alone.

The branches of the plum tree outside scraped against the wall. The leaves rustled. After a while I began to suspect that someone might be creeping up the wall, to try and get in here after me. Finally I could stand the suspense no longer, gave up my post and crept back across the bedroom floor and on down the stairs.

As I reached for the door handle, somebody must have heard me, and pulled open the door. Losing my balance I fell off the third stair, landing on hands and knees on the living room floor. 'N-n-n-nothing to report,' I whispered, half crying with shock, 'I c-c-c-couldn't see a thing.'

'No, I didn't think you would,' muttered my mother. 'I really don't think I can stand this uncertainty any longer, I'm going to open the door and demand to know, who it is and what they want. They have been creeping out there quite long enough. For all we know they might be setting a fuse or something, planning to blow

76

the house up and us with it. I think it's time we found out exactly what's going on.

'Oh no don't,' we cried as she went determinedly to the door, anxious for her safety and of course our own, but nothing would dissuade her. 'Keep well back,' she ordered, then with a heavy poker held ready to defend herself with if necessary, she carefully turned the handle, pulling the door open a fraction, when nothing happened she opened it a bit more.

'Who are you?' Mother called nervously, 'What do you want?' There was an ominous silence. 'Who are you?' she shouted, 'Stop hiding out there and make yourself known.' The door was pulled open wider. We children crept forwards to have a look. Then slowly a form materialized from the darkness and stepped towards us, uttering a loud plaintive, 'Moo, Moo-oo. It was a big black and white cow!

It so startled us. We nearly jumped out of our skins in fright. Just before it reached the door my mother with great presence of mind slammed it shut. The relief that it was a cow and not a German paratrooper was so intense, I didn't know whether to laugh or cry. Nobody said anything till the lamp had been relit, then hearing a disgruntled 'Moo-Moo-oo' from outside the door we turned to each other and roared with laughter.

When father returned home not long after, I asked tongue in cheek, 'I don't suppose you met up with any German Paratroopers when you were out?'

'No I didn't,' he answered giving me a peculiar look. 'I have been too busy helping to round up a heard of dairy cows. The wind blew their gate open and they got loose, most of them came down this way, did you see anything of them?'

Well that explained the footsteps and the coughs, for as anyone living in the countryside knows, when you pass a heard of cows in a field at night, they sometimes cough or clear their throats like humans.

However there was never an explanation for the so called church bells. We thought it could have been two pieces of metal banging together in the wind, the resulting noise sounding like church bells in the distance.

Father was devastated when he saw the state of his garden next morning. All his greens eaten off, everything else trampled to the ground. He ranted and raved, about what he would do and say to the farmer when he saw him. He would sue him for compensation and goodness knows what else. For a while the air was blue, then it slowly began to clear and a smile came to his face, as with spade and bucket, he went round collecting up the many 'pancakes' that were scattered everywhere. Little did we know he had some young plants in a green house just dying for the manure he had now acquired.

Chapter 7 The Entertainment.

A little village social evening had been organized. It was to be held at the school. I, who was good at dressing up and impersonating people, was, to my great surprise asked to do an act. I was going to be a professor and speak about various well known people from the village. My father who was brilliant at drawing, now drew me comical pictures of the chosen few on postcards.

The idea was that I should say a word or two about each individual, mimic them, then hand the picture to a helper behind me, who would hang it on the wall so other people could come and look at it. It went well, I attended three practice sessions and looked forward to the great night.

I was filled with excitement when the day arrived. The 'tools of my trade' as my mother called them were packed in a small attaché case. Clasping it in one hand, I raced off to meet up with Jane, a woman who was helping arrange things. I was to accompany her to the school.

The village people began arriving. All determined to support a local function and the social began. Everyone was enjoying themselves dancing and singing, with various acts in between, when a lorry load of soldiers appeared. They were 'our boys' and people made them welcome.

However soon after came two lorry loads of American airmen. They were welcomed also, but our poor little school room wasn't made for so many. People were packed in like sardines, hardly able to move when they danced, nowhere to sit comfortably and the air was full of cigarette smoke.

When the time came to do my act, people constantly brushed against the chair I had been given to stand on, several times it tipped. I became nervous and frightened, voices were shouting, 'We don't want any more rubbish, we want dancing, dancing, dancing.'

Most of the airmen had had too much to drink before coming to us and were merry. One was drawing everyone's attention by throwing ten shilling notes into the air and laughing with merriment, as he watched people scrabbling for them. Things were getting out of hand. The locals were fed up after all their efforts, for this was just a small village social evening, not a dance hall.

Suddenly in the midst of the uproar, an elderly woman stood up and in a beautiful compelling voice began to sing. 'Eternal Father, strong to save, who's arm doth bind the restless waves.' 'Why, that's Mrs Falton,' whispered a voice from behind me. 'Used to sing on the stage you know'

The golden voice sang on, gradually everyone in the school room became silent. All eyes turned towards her. The Americans seemed mesmerized, then slowly, a few at a time, they vanished through the door, our lads following soon after. No one really noticed them go, so intent were they on our friend with the beautiful voice.

As she finished she said 'That was for our husbands and sons, uncles and nephews and for all the other brave men out there on the sea, in peril day and night from submarines, bombs, mines and guns. Now I shall sing, 'Abide with me,' for all our brave lads in the Royal Air Force and in the Army.' As she sang there wasn't a dry eye in the school room. I was only a small child but I stared at this beautiful woman who I had never seen before and found tears coursing down my cheeks, at those beautiful moving words.

As the singing came to the end, there was such a thunderous applause. Never in my whole life, had I heard anything like it. 'Encore, Encore,' shouted the adults,
'More, More,' shouted the children.

Mrs Felton smiled, a little embarrassed at her reception. 'Just one more then my dears, but this time I want you all to join in and sing with me.' She waved her arms to include everybody. 'We are going to raise the roof. Are you ready? There'll always be an England and England shall be free'. The voices raised in unison, it was so loud I looked up to see if the roof really was being raised,

I didn't know whether to be pleased or sorry when I realised it wasn't.

How the people loved it. Once more came that thunderous applause, that went on and on and on, until I thought it would never end. It did abruptly though, when someone noticed a couple of ARP members standing just inside the door. 'Sorry to interrupt', called one, 'Thought you would like to know there is a raid on. Siren went about twenty minutes ago, there's been a lot of gunfire along the coast and one or two Jerry planes droning over.'

'Your lights are alright at the moment. We checked. Make sure nobody shows a light of any description as you leave. No cigarettes, matches or torches please.' As they slipped back through the door, the scene in the schoolroom was chaotic. People collected coats and other belongings and began to leave hurriedly.

All interest had gone from the social, only one thought was in their minds, that of getting home to their families. Most of the lights had already been extinguished. Everywhere was dim. I managed to grab my coat and small attaché case and looked round for Jane.

There she was over near the door. As I made my way towards her, there came a sudden surge of people. The remaining lights went out, I was carried out through the door into the dark of the night, across the playground where I tried to stop, but was pushed on relentlessly. It must have been on the verge outside the school that a push from behind made me slip and I fell headlong. My case shot out of my hand, I must have been winded, for by the time I had recovered, felt round on my hands and knees for my case and risen to my feet, there was nobody about. It was as if they had all been dissolved into the darkness.

I was utterly terrified. I felt like screaming and crying but what would be the use, there was nobody to hear me. Sniffing back the tears, I realised I hadn't much choice. I either stood here in the dark all night until I was found, or I started walking home.

This was going to be easier said than done, for I was in a world of my own, a very frightening world of darkness. How could all those people have gone so quickly, there wasn't even the remotest sound anywhere.

A lone Dornier droned overhead, but he was so high up I didn't worry about him. A few bangs sounded in the distance, then a flash or two danced across the sky. A searchlight flickered up, wavered and vanished again. I was alone, no bikes, no people, nothing.

Slowly I walked along, trying to keep close to the verge. Now and again there was a rustle in the hedgerow beside me. It was no use panicking. I couldn't see to run anywhere. Eventually I turned off the main road and into the lane, remembering there was a deep ditch on one side and a prickly hedge on the other.

Try as I might, I couldn't walk in a straight line, time and time again finding myself on the grass verge and not knowing how I got there. When eventually I heard heavy footsteps approaching. I was petrified and stood rooted to the spot, my legs so weak I couldn't have run if the need had arisen.

My mouth opened and an uncontrollable sound issued forth. 'Is that you?' called my mother's anxious voice. Thankfully I answered. She cried out 'Thank God.'
Jane had been pushed aside also by the crowd. Hearing running footsteps in front of her, she had presumed it was me, so had gone back to where she lived. My mother waiting there for me had become concerned when Jane had come home alone. Being frightened herself she had taken long strides and thumped her feet down as she walked, so that if anyone was hanging about up to no good, they would think she was a man.

Chapter 8 The Aluminium Aeroplane.

'Be attentive children,' scolded our teacher 'and listen very carefully to what I have to say. Next week there will be a campaign on to collect articles made of aluminium. When melted down the resulting product will be used to make new aircraft. I want you all to go home now and over the weekend ask your parents, friends and relatives if they have anything to spare. Saucepans in particular are needed. Large or small ones, bent or broken, holed or whole. If you can't find saucepans, don't worry there are plenty of other things made from aluminium that you can collect, such as coat hangers, colanders, shoetrees, jelly moulds. You might find a thimble or two or various ornaments. We need anything and everything you can find made out of aluminium, so go home now and start turning out those cupboards. Hunt through those sheds and outhouses. Search high and low, you'll be surprised at what you can find.

All the things you collect may be brought to school on any day next week. I have compiled a list of names, so whatever you bring each day will be counted. For instance if you bring one article a number one will be put against your name and so forth. At the end of the week we will count up to see who has worked the hardest and brought the most. We will crown that person the aluminium king or queen for the day and that person will be granted certain privileges. Have a busy weekend children. Who knows we might be able to collect enough to make a whole aeroplane. Don't forget now our country is relying on you. It needs you and your aluminium.'

Chattering excitedly I dashed home with my friends. We discussed with each other where we would go collecting as we did not want to go to the same houses. As soon as I arrived home I told my mother all about the campaign for collecting aluminium to make aeroplanes with.

Mother laughed and said 'Before you ask, I've got nothing to give you, nothing that I can spare, so don't count on me for anything. To be honest I could do with one or two new saucepans myself. Two of mine have already got pot menders in the bottom.'

I could hardly wait to finish my tea, so eager was I to get off and make a start collecting before anyone else took my pitch. Maybe, I mused as I went along, if I got a lot of saucepans, I could spare my mother one or two. With this uppermost in my mind, I ran along the lane to visit the home of an elderly deaf spinster who lived in a cottage near a wood.

Knowing as I did that she was a deaf as a post, I gave a good knock on the front door. Waited patiently for a few seconds then banged again, loud enough I thought to awaken the dead, let alone a deaf old lady. Afterwards as I sucked my sore knuckles I heard a door open inside. 'Alright, alright, I'm coming,' shouted a very irate voice. 'Some people don't seem to have a minute to live.' A key was turned in the lock and the door was opened slowly to reveal a tall white haired woman dressed entirely in black.

The lady was surprised to see me, peering down at me through her spectacles as if I was something the cat had brought in. 'A kid, hmmm, I might have known. What do you want banging on my door like that? It was you wasn't it?' I nodded apprehensively. She looked so angry my whole body shook right down to my toes in fright.
Somehow I managed to say, 'Please have you any saucepans?'
'What's that?' she bellowed. 'Speak up so I can hear what it is that you want?' 'Saucepans,' I shouted frantically, 'Have you got any saucepans.
'Saucepans, did you say saucepans?' she put a hand to her ear and leaned towards me. 'Yes of course I've got saucepans, what else do you think I cook my food in, hey?'
'I meant to say,' I was becoming more and more confused by the second. 'Have you got any to spare, I want some to help build an aeroplane with.'
'To build what?' she roared. 'An aeroplane you say?' she stared at me then she laughed. A horrible cackling sort of laugh, 'Why bless me, a silly little slip of a thing like you, build an aeroplane, don't talk such nonsense don't,' and the door was slammed in my face.

Well it was no use giving up at my first rejection I thought, so, somewhat subdued, I skipped along the road to visit the next house on my list. I had no luck there either, nor at the following one. Feeling angry and disheartened I walked away. Somehow I had thought people would fall over themselves to give me saucepans they did not want. I had no idea that the collecting of this so called aluminium was going to be such hard and tedious work.

Noticing a farmhouse in the distance, I wondered whether to try my luck there. It was so far out I was certain no one else would bother to call. By the time I arrived at my destination after running all the way, I was quite worn out. Pausing for a second to get my breath, my hand reached out for the latch on the big, wooden white painted gate, then with shock I realised that I had company.

A big white Billy-Goat stood like a sentinel just inside, sniffing at me inquisitively. I shot back in a hurry, then further as he stood on his hind legs and rested his front legs on the bars of the gate. His little piggy eyes stared at me unblinkingly, the beards on his chin waggling as he moved position slightly. My fright was renewed. I thought he was preparing to jump over the gate after me. I didn't like the look of him at all. It was the closest I have ever been to a Billy-Goat before and I had no wish to get better acquainted.

I pretended to run off down the road, then after waiting a few minutes, crept back on tiptoe and hid myself in the hedge, wondering what to do for the best. I badly wanted some saucepans to take to school on Monday and felt I couldn't go home after coming all this way without at least knocking on the door and asking.

Feeling braver, I peered over the gate. There was no sign of the goat, anyway as I tried to tell myself, I wasn't afraid of a little Billy Goat was I? The gate opened easily enough and down the yard I marched, though I must admit, it was not very confidently. Halfway along I heard a noise behind me and peered back, Mr Billy Goat with his head tucked down was racing down the farmyard after me, hell bent on causing mischief.

Clasping my bottom with both hands because I thought it was the most vulnerable part of me, I took to my heels and ran, absolutely terrified. It felt as if the devil was after me. Taking advantage of the first available cover, which was a large trellis work completely covered by rambler roses, I managed to dodge behind it, heard the goat skid to a halt, then he ambled in after me.

A stifled scream forced its way out, as I backed away gradually one step at a time. I felt something solid behind my back. It was the door of a nearby shed. Keeping my eye on the goat, I fumbled for the latch, lifted it and then pulled the door open just enough for me to slip inside. Drawing it shut with a bang I leaned against it thankfully and thought I was safe at last.

My peace did not last very long for a faint sound from the interior of the shed had me whirling round in terror. Was that old goat so determined to get me, he had got in another way? To my amazement it wasn't the goat, it was an old gentleman sitting on a lavatory seat with his trousers down around his ankles. I don't know who was more surprised him or me. How embarrassing it was. I just did not know where to look.

He recovered first. 'Wasser matta little ow'd gal?' He sounded ámused and his voice, though gruff was kind. 'Wass the old goat arter ya? Old bugger he be sometimes is owd Bill, but he oon't hart ya gal, not iffen ya tarn and face im'. When I made no answer he laughed. 'Sceered are ya? Can't say I blame ya, niver ya mind little un, iffen yowd loike to turn ya back, and yowd betta howd your snout as well, ull help ya'.

I saw no alternative. I certainly hadn't the courage to go and face that monster on my own. I turned my back discreetly and held my nose as instructed, listening meanwhile to the grunts and the tearing of newspaper behind me.

Presently a hand rested on my shoulder, it propelled me out of the door, where I came face to face with Owd Bill, who was patiently waiting for his prey to emerge. 'Bin up ter ya tricks again have ya, ya owd rascal?' chuckled the man. 'Well clear orf ya sorft Owd fule, ya fritted this poor we gal, she's as white as a bit of Irish bed linen. Proper affeared a animiles loik yew she is.'

Still with his hand on my shoulder he guided in the direction of the gate, without asking me why I was there, or what I wanted. I dare not say anything. I was too petrified with Owd Bill walking just behind me. When we reached the gate he waved me through, then closed it behind me. Raising his hand in farewell he walked back down the yard again without a backward glance. The goat trotting beside him like a dog. I watched them out of sight, then very disappointedly, and still with no saucepans, ran home.

I was greeted by my sister Jean who shouted, 'Hey, how many saucepans did you get?' Not wanting to say none, in front of everyone I replied,
'Hundreds and hundreds, so many I couldn't bring them all home. I'm to go back tomorrow to fetch them.'
'In that case' said grandma 'you won't need the two old bent ones I've got in my shed, I'll give them to somebody else, somebody who hasn't got any.'
'Oh no please,' I was nearly in tears. 'I haven't got any, I only said that, I've been laughed at by an old woman who was deaf and lives near a wood. Refused point blank at two other houses and then chased by an old Billy Goat at a farm. I was scared it was going to butt me or whatever goats do, so I hid in the shed, only to discover it wasn't a shed it was a lavatory and it was occupied by an old man with his trousers down. If you only knew what a terrible time I have had you wouldn't all sit there laughing at me.' After listening to my tale of woe they all laughed even more.

On Monday morning I was up early. Clutching an old bent saucepan in each hand I set off to school, thrilled that I had two and lots of children didn't have any. The teacher took my offering, threw them onto a heap in the playground and placed a two next to my name.

An older girl then arrived with some things in a hessian sack, which she tipped out onto the ground with a clatter, looking round at us, I thought with a rather smug smile. The girl had a five put by her name. Everyone felt very envious, especially when on the next morning she brought some more.

Day after day the pile of aluminium grew bigger. We roamed the fields and hunted along the hedges and ditches. To our delight we found several old saucepans that had been thrown away. Then, when we searched an old pit where people threw their rubbish, we found several more. I washed mine carefully in my mother's water butt, when she wasn't looking and took them to school. Soon I had a seven placed next to my name. I was so pleased with myself. On the last day most children had saved something to take, and our old friend as usual had brought more. She was of course crowned with a silver paper crown, Queen of Aluminium and allowed to do what she wanted for the rest of the day, much to the disappointment of the rest of us.

When we arrived home from the school grandma was there. She wanted to know who was crowned queen, and all the details. When we had related the day to her she told us a little story that another member of the Women's Voluntary Service (WVS) had told them at their latest meeting.

Apparently in a nearby village, on the last day of a collection of aluminium, a child who had been bringing rather a lot of saucepans, colanders, aluminium bowls, fish slices and other things, had brought still more. The teacher was just congratulating the girl on her great effort when voices were heard, loud angry voices, and through the school gates marched three women one behind the other.

In the lead was an old lady wearing a bright red beret, which had somehow slipped forward over one eye. The lady's grey almost white hair was still done up in rag curlers, the ends hanging down like rat's tails swinging this way and that as she moved her head. An angry scowl was set on her face, and a walking stick brandished menacingly in her gnarled hands. Behind her the other two women were shouting incoherently and waving their arms.

Immediately thinking they were three mad lunatics escaped from the asylum, the teacher quickly ushered the children inside and then went to speak to them. Ten minutes later the child who had brought all the things was called outside, later another child was crowned King of the Aluminium.

Well, no secrets last for ever. We soon discovered that the three women were the girl's mother, granny and aunt. They lived in three houses all next door to each other. Aunt and granny had been away for a week, so the child had no chance to ask them if they had anything made of aluminium to spare. She took her mothers keys to her aunt's and granny's houses, then went through their kitchen cupboards, bringing just about all they possessed in the way of kitchen utensils made of aluminium.

The three ladies kicked up such a fuss. Blaming the teacher for asking the children to bring aluminium to school, not the girl for taking it from their cupboards. They threatened to report her to the school governors, to the vicar and the police if she didn't allow them to search for their things. They apparently spent the entire weekend, transferring items from one pile to another, in a desperate attempt to find their belongings.

Chapter 9 Branches.

Mother cycled slowly along, a worried frown on her brow. Would the coalman come again soon? She hoped so; the coal in the shed was dangerously low. What would she do if he didn't come before she ran out? She relied on the old cooking range; she had nothing else to cook with, then she mused, in these dull dark days of war, the poor coal man can't come if he has no coal to deliver, it was a vicious circle.

Mother was startled out of her reminiscing, as a man ran out of a field gateway calling urgently for her to stop. 'Hang on a minute Ma'am,' he puffed, 'we are cutting trees down along side the road here. One is due down any second, I daren't run the risk of allowing you to continue, just in case it falls the wrong way and goes across the road, as you're pedalling past.'

He seemed a nice friendly sort of chap and stood chatting while they waited. Soon a distant shout was heard; a giant tree slowly toppled over and struck the ground with a mighty crash. 'There you are' smiled the man looking relieved, 'You can be on your way again now. Sorry if I delayed you, but it was better to be safe than sorry.'
'Just a minute,' she said as he began to walk away, ' I know you take the trunk and any large branches that are of any use to you, but what happens to the remainder, you know, the smaller branches and bits and pieces?'

'Anything of no use we burn ma'am, we burn it up out of the way, because we like to leave the place clean and tidy when we take the trunks away.'
'You burn it?' gasped my mother in shocked disbelief. 'What a wicked waste, when there are people like me who could make good use of that wood. What with coal in short supply, an invalid husband and three daughters, goodness knows how I am going to keep them warm this winter.'

He looked perplexed staring at her in deep thought, he then removed his cap to scratch the back of his head, 'So you could do with some wood to burn then Ma'am. If I let you have some, how would you get it home?'

'Borrow a wheelbarrow,' came her prompt reply, 'getting it home will pose no problem, we don't live very far away.'

As if making up his mind he said, ' Better come with me then my dear,' and off he strode. Hastily leaning her bike against the gate she followed him into the nearby field. She could hear the sound of men's voices clearly now and the sound of a saw as branches were detached from the newly fallen trunk. Several other trees, already felled, lay on the ground and it was to one of these that the man made his way.

He stopped and turned, clearing his throat loudly, 'Now then Ma'am, if I said you could have all the branches and wood from around this tree, would you be able to clear it?'
'I most certainly could', she declared, 'when can I start?'

'Tonight I suppose,' he chuckled. 'We should be finished felling by then. Will one tree be enough or can you clear two?'
'Two please,' she replied without hesitation, her eyes gleaming with excitement.
'Right,' he said, 'This tree and the next one are yours, I'll give you ten days to clear your wood, when we come to collect the trunks what you haven't taken we'll burn. By the way, if you know of anyone else who would be glad of some wood, tell them to come and see me, I shall be here until about five o'clock tonight,'

After tendering her thanks my mother cycled home in great excitement. Then she almost ran over to Grandma's house. Minutes later Grandma wheeled her bike out of the shed and pedalled off, as did a couple of neighbours mother met on her way home. Soon the trees were all taken.

That evening we went to have a look at what we now called, our trees. My mother went prepared with saw and axe, pushing them there in my sister's old pushchair. My sister Eliza and I played happily amongst the branches and climbed onto the trunk to run along it. My mother picked up the big chips of wood from both trees, that the men had chopped out before commencing to fell the trunk. She then set to work with saw and axe.

91

'If the wood could be cut into manageable lengths and carried home, it could be sawn into suitably sized pieces for the fire when needed,' she muttered, ' The main thing is to get it home.'

All too soon it was getting dark and time to leave. The push chair was loaded with pieces of wood and the bags filled with wood chips, tied to the back. How my mother pushed it home I shall never know, for I tried and couldn't move it. But I did at her request drag a big branch behind me. It was so big it swept the narrow lane on both sides as I went by.

Next morning we were at the field early, my mother determined to get as much wood home as possible. She hadn't been able to borrow a wheelbarrow as planned, because the owners themselves were now using them, to bring their own wood home. So the pushchair would have to do.

I had taken my mother's bicycle this morning and was soon on my way home dragging another twiggy branch behind me. On my third trip my mother remembered the old pram in the shed at home. 'If you feel strong enough do get it out and bring it back with you,' she said. 'We'll load that up.'

My sister Jean was home. She helped me get out the pram, then not wanting to walk back to the fields with it, we found some pieces of string and towed it behind the two bicycles. While the pram was being loaded up with several large thick pieces of wood we saw a bicycle go by. It was ridden by an elderly woman called Miss Mary, who lived in a big house in the village. Miss Mary stared as she passed, probably wondering what all the activity in the field was about, for the neighbours and Grandma were there as well.

Miss Mary was stretching her neck she peered back for one last look, as she turned the corner. It was fatal, for the bicycle slid along side the high bank and some how deposited Miss Mary on the top, there she sat in the long, damp grass, still staring over to see what we were doing.

'Ooooooh, I expect she'll have wet knickers sitting up there.' I giggled.

'Hush,' said my mother with a little chuckle herself. 'Come on, it's time you two girls pushed that pram home for me.'

Meanwhile a neighbour had rushed across to Miss Mary, who still sat there as if stunned. He held out his hand to help her down. 'Are you alright miss?' he asked in a concerned voice. Obviously in shock she declined to answer him, but took the proffered hand and clambered down the bank. Picking up the bicycle he held it while she climbed on, then ran with her a little way to give her a push off.

As she pedalled out of sight Jean and I were preparing to depart for home with the loaded pram. We made slow progress to start with, the strings cutting into our hands leaving deep ruts. Then we wrapped the strings round our sleeves and that was better. Soon we picked up speed, laughing and singing, 'It's all Hitler's fault, we haven't got no coal and all because he's a silly old fool.'

The pram rumbled along behind us. One wheel had developed an awesome screech, and the springs were protesting with creaks and groans, at the unaccustomed weight. Poor Miss Mary must have wondered what on earth was coming up behind her.

My sister in her fright, thinking there was going to be a terrible disaster, dropped her string and shot ahead. Without her help and guidance the pram veered across the road, pushing against the back of my bike. I had no control over it as I slid across the road, over a deep rut and then flew over the handlebars into a freshly ploughed field. The pram turned over behind me, disgorging its load.

Groaning, I lifted my face out of the soft clinging earth and spat out dirt. From a distance I heard my sister saying, 'So you're not dead after all, then my advice to you is get up, I hope you realize what you've done.'
'Don't know. What have I done?' I mumbled, spitting out more dirt.
'Look up the field and you'll see,' she snapped. So I struggled to a sitting position and squinted round. A little way back sat Miss Mary, looking quite comfortable perched on top of a furrow her bicycle beside her.

'Get up! Stir your stumps,' hissed my sister, prodding me with her foot. 'Go and see if she's alright and for goodness sake, apologise to her for knocking her off her bike.' 'What?' I gasped, cringing at the thought. ' No, not me, I'm going to load this wood up again, when you've helped me right the pram, then I'm going to pull it home.'
'Oh no you're not!' she roared, clutching my arm and turning me in the direction of Miss Mary. ' Its useless us loading up that wood, until we know if she is alright, because you never know when people get old. If she's hurt, we might have to push her home in the pram.'

Slowly and reluctantly, with lagging footsteps, I made my way back up the field. My heart missed a beat as I approached Miss Mary, for the poor woman's shoulders were heaving, her hands covered her face, as if she was sobbing her heart out. Oh dear, I'm going to get terribly wrong for this I thought. My life isn't going to be worth living. She must be hurt ever so bad.

Finally, after standing in front of her for several minutes, trying to pluck up the courage to say something, she looked up, raised her hand and pointed at me, then went off almost into hysterics. Which made me wonder if she might have struck her head and gone a bit potty.

But when I returned home later, I realised I must have looked a sight, for the dirt was still caked on my face like a mudpack. Trembling in my shoes I muttered, 'Excuse me,' then a little louder, 'Excuse me, you're not in agony or anything I hope.'
'Ha ha, ha,' she roared, 'funniest thing I've seen in years. You trundling along with that aged perambulator; it going out of your control, careering across the road and you, ha, ha, ha. You taking off like a bird, soaring up over the handle bars of your bicycle and coming down to earth, to bury your head in the dirt like an ostrich. Then, ha, ha, ha, the aged perambulator tipping right over and shedding it's load. Oh, oh,' she clutched her stomach, and then went off into another paroxysm of laughter.

I had to stand by helplessly as she laughed herself silly, Further down the road I could see my sister waiting patiently. She had righted the pram and was no doubt wondering if it was going to be needed to transport Miss Mary home. Until she was sure, she daren't start loading it up again. But eventually the laughter eased slightly. Always the Jack Blunt I burst out, 'Are you going to sit there all day Miss?' I had to ask three times before she finally held up one arm; I grasped it and helped her to her feet.

Spasms of laughter still shook her bony frame as she began to brush herself down. Meanwhile I picked up her tall, old-fashioned bicycle, straightened the basket on the front and pushed it onto the road, where I stood waiting impatiently.

Satisfied at last, she suddenly bent to pick up her red hat, that had lain there half buried and unnoticed. The sight of that hat sent my brain working, what was it I had heard about people who wore a red hat? Oh yes, red hat no underwear, but surely not Miss Mary? She was much too dignified.

Thump, she rammed the offending, red, felt object onto the top of my head. 'Here you are, you can have this, it matches your face. Ha, ha, ha,' she broke into a peals of laughter again, accepted the bicycle from me and after two or three attempts, got on and wobbled off down the road, As she passed my sister waiting by the pram, there came a maniacal outbreak of laughter. My sister thought the woman was demented.

It took a great deal of effort to reload the pram. Somehow we managed it between us, then wheeled it home. When my mother found out about what had happened, she was absolutely horrified. 'Good Heavens,' she stormed at us, ' you two could have killed the poor woman. After that, we weren't allowed to tow the pram behind our bicycles any more. We had to push it.

Over the next few days, we all worked hard to fetch the wood home, my mother harder than most. While we were at school, she leaned the heavy, thick, long pieces over the handlebars and seat of her bicycle and wheeled them back that way. We were all so relieved when the hard work was finished and all the wood safely gathered in. When the cold weather arrived and the snow lay on the ground, we were able to reap the benefit of all that arduous effort and stoke our fire up with an unlimited supply of wood.

Chapter 10 The Countryside Evacuation

I didn't mind being transferred to another school. In fact I was rather looking forward to it, but I was so very disappointed when my school bicycle arrived. Instead of a nice new one as expected, it was an old one that had been done up. What's more, mine looked older and more dilapidated than any of the others that two men in a lorry had just delivered.

Catching a glimpse of my face as I read the label on the bike, to make sure it was the one meant for me, the teacher said, 'Take that expression off your face child. You can't expect a new bicycle. There's a war on now you know. It's far more important, to build a new aeroplane, tank or gun to fight the Germans with, than present you with a new bicycle.'

I soon got over my disappointment, for having a bicycle of my own, even if it wasn't a brand new one, was better than no bike at all. On my way to school, I would meet my friend Carol who didn't live quite as far away as I did and who had her own bicycle. We'd cycle on together.

We thought the world of each other, having both started school on the same day. As two shy five year olds we had somehow clung together and been bosom pals throughout junior school. But alas, all good things come to an end.

The post lady had paid us a visit, whilst father was standing outside. He came indoors looking extremely pleased with himself. Turning an envelope over in his hands he read out loud, ' On His Majesty's Service.' Chuckling he said, 'Goodness gracious me, I know what this is, after all this time. The government has decided they can't win this war without my help.'

'Never,' he said shaking his head, 'did I think I'd see the day. First they didn't call me up to join the services, and then when I applied and offered myself, they turned me down flat. Now by the looks of this envelope, they want me. They must have some special sort of job to offer me.'

'Something important really important, it must be. I reckon it's a desk job. In that case they are bound to promote me, make me officer,' he joked. 'A Colonel at least, unless of course the Prime Minister is retiring and they want me to fill the vacancy.'

Looking at my father and the happy smile on his face I thought, if they are his calling up papers, then my prayers had been answered. I hoped it wouldn't be too long before he went. I was fed up with getting wrong, being picked on, blamed for everything that happened. Mind you, I'm not disagreeing with the fact that he had just cause sometimes.

'Don't you think it would be a good idea to open that envelope before you go jumping to conclusions?' asked my mother who had been hovering near. 'It could be anything.'
'I know what it is,' he snapped. 'I've seen calling up papers before, still,' he glanced round at our eager faces. 'None of you will be satisfied until I open it, so you can see for yourselves.'

Jean, anticipating his need had fetched a knife. He took it, slitting open the envelope and withdrawing the letter. Glancing smugly around at us all, he unfolded it and began to read. Quickly we saw his face tighten, and then gradually whiten. Without a word he passed the letter to my mother. Reaching for a chair behind him, he sat down as if in a state of shock.

Three pairs of enquiring eyes transferred themselves from father to mother. Mother read the letter through twice, shook her head as she looked up and said, 'I can't believe what I'm reading. It says here we have got to move. Find somewhere else to live because the Admiralty needs this area for a Battle Zone.'

Jean was the first to recover; incredulity then sheer delight flitted across her face. 'Good,' she shouted excitedly. 'When can we go?' I gasped in horror,
'But I don't want to go!' I yelled, 'I don't want to leave here, not see grandma, grandfather, auntie and all my friends.'

This seemed to anger my sister. 'Just because you don't want to go, it doesn't mean other people don't. We could have a nice new house, bigger and better than this one, find new friends and in a few months you wouldn't want to come back here.'

'Oh yes I would,' I snapped, beginning to feel quite upset.
'Stop bickering!' shouted father irritably. 'Just be quiet and let me think. Bad news like this needs careful consideration. For instance, where would we get another house with rent we can afford, a bigger and better house would mean a higher rent, it's all we can do to pay for this place.'

My mother looked thoughtful. 'I don't like the sound of this.' She waved the letter. 'Why on earth would the Admiralty need our house? I think I'd better slip next door and have a word with Annie, see if she can throw any light on the situation.'

As she stepped outside the door, she spotted another neighbour hurrying along, waving an envelope, so she waved ours. Both letter were identical. While they talked Auntie came half running down the path, a worried expression on her lined and wrinkled face. She too was clutching an envelope tightly in her hand.

'My dears,' she greeted them, 'what do you think?' Auntie spotted their envelopes and said 'Oh you've both got one. Whatever is going on? Fancy us all having to move house because the government wants our land. Surely to goodness they could find somewhere more suitable. Incidentally, dear, your mother has got one of those too. She was coming over with me, but she had a visitor.'

Our neighbour's friend now came cycling up. 'Snap.' he chuckled, producing an identical envelope.
'What' gasped our neighbour 'not you as well? I thought it might just apply to our little corner here.'
'Good God, no man,' declared the old man, his handle bar moustache twitching. 'It's the whole of the bloody parish. All down the other end where I live have all got notice to quit. On my way here I passed numerous little groups of people, huddled together and waving their envelopes, wondering what to do and how to go about it. They say it's like a bolt out of the blue.'

There was a long silence now as they stood digesting this latest information, wondering what their next course of action would be. 'Any ideas?' asked our neighbours. 'According to our letters, we only have four weeks.'

'There are a lot of us to find new homes,' wailed Auntie worriedly. 'Supposing we can't find anywhere to move into, what then? They can't just turn us out, can they?'
'I really don't know,' mother shook her head. 'I would hardly think so, but then again, if they really are that desperate to get us out, they would have to turn us out, if it's only into a camp somewhere. I don't know about you others but I don't fancy living under canvas with the winter coming on, a nice warm Nissen hut would be better.'

'Why don't we all go next door and see Annie, I expect if she has one of these letters she's sitting there feeling as if a bomb has hit her. Annie was sobbing her heart out, 'Just you look together,' she cried with a loud sniff. 'Look what I had come through the post this morning. This letter says I have got to move out of my house.'

'So have we all,' declared Auntie sadly, sinking into the nearest chair.
'We have all got a letter,' moaned my mother. 'Every one of us and as far as we know, everyone in the whole village.'
'Oh dear oh dear,' mumbled another woman who had just joined them. I'm in the family way and my man is in the forces, God knows where. Supposing we have to go away and he can't find me when he comes home.'

'I don't want to go anywhere,' sniffed Annie, 'I want to stay here. This is my home and my little bit of land. I've worked hard for it over the years. My man is buried in the churchyard, so are other members of my family. When my time comes, I want to be buried there too, not to have to lay beside strangers in some far off distant village.'

Auntie jumped up. 'We know who is to blame for all this, don't we?' she declared venomously. 'It's that bloody old Hitler. If it wasn't for him there would be none of this trouble and worry. What wouldn't I do, for the chance to have a go at him, with my husband's double - barrelled shotgun. 'I'd pepper his trousers I would!'

'You are not the only one,' Annie leaned forward in her chair and held both hands out in front of her. 'Just give me a frying pan in my hand and put him in front of me.' She thumped her arms up and down. 'I'll pulverize him, knock him into the ground and stamp on him, the wicked inhuman brute, son of Satan that's what he is.'

Smiles spread over the worried faces. The situation was so comical, as they listened to these two elderly ladies, normally so calm and reasonable, give vent to bitter resentment and rage. It ended up with them all having a good laugh, which relieved their feelings slightly. They split up soon afterwards, promising to let each other know if there were any further developments.

My friend Carol and I discussed the situation at school. She mentioned her father was terribly worried. Being cowman at the farm where he worked, he had said the farmer was angry and broken-hearted at being given notice to move out, leaving his fields full of lovingly tended crops.

The worry of finding another farm and transporting his dairy herd and other farm animals to goodness knows where, had filled him with such a despondency. He didn't think he could leave his life's work and start again at his age. If the worst came to the worst, he would sell up and retire.

As the days passed, the odd one or two people in the village managed to find somewhere else to live. These few packed their belongings and departed, but the majority had found nowhere.

Advertisements in the local papers were carefully scrutinized. People got out their bikes and pedalled miles on excursions into the countryside, or nearby towns and villages. Always hopeful, they might come across a house to let. They wrote to people they knew and relatives. Word was passed by mouth. The villagers were getting desperate. It wasn't only the problem of finding somewhere to live. Work for those fit and able also had to be taken into consideration.

Then right out of the blue, Carol dropped her bombshell. 'I don't know how to tell you this,' she was nearly in tears. 'My dad has found another job, with a vacant farm cottage, the farmer needs

someone straight away, so we are leaving this Saturday'.
'What? I burst out, 'but it's only two days away.'
We had been friends all these years. I had never ever thought about the possibility of us one day being separated. I burst into tears, for our friendship was something special. We threw our arms around each other sobbing our hearts out. 'I shan't be coming to school anymore' she finally uttered in a wobbly voice, 'I've got to stop at home and help my mother pack,'

I never saw her again. Carol wrote once to say they had arrived and she missed me, but there was another girl living down the road from her, whom she thought she could be friends with, and that was that.

My mother, like most people in the parish had begun to pack. Her few precious good pieces of china were wrapped in newspaper and placed carefully in a box. Cupboards were turned out. Anything no longer needed was placed in a heap near the back door. It grew bigger every day. Clothes not being worn were stuffed in a homemade sack with a drawstring at the top. Books were tied in bundles. Coal was shovelled into bags. Favourite flowers dug up and placed in old tins or buckets, all ready to go at a few hour's notice. According to father that might be all the warning we would get.

When I was clearing out the shed one evening, it was suggested I fill the old pram with the rubbish, wheel it up the road to a disused pit and dump it. I agreed but I was most indignant when I saw what was being thrown out.

'Not that dear old pushchair?' I screeched. 'Why it's got two good wheels on it. I get a lot of fun playing with that. My dress, my favourite,' I held it up against me feeling absolutely horrified.
'That's too small for you' grunted my mother, 'besides it's torn down the back.'

'But I like it,' I said and clutched it to me. 'Just look at poor old Topsy doll laying there! I know she only has one arm and one leg and her eyes won't stay in position for any length of time, but I shan't get a wink of sleep if I know she is laying down the pit with all the rubbish.'

101

'What's the tin bath doing there? How are we going to have a bath if you throw that away?' My mother sighed in exasperation, 'For goodness sake child, I don't want the bath because Annie next door is giving me another one. Ours has a tiny hole in it, if you remember.'

'Yes but,' I was so insistent. 'The old one will come in handy won't it? I can't take that down to the pit, it's too good. You'll be able to pack some of your things in it when we move, won't you? That is, if we find anywhere to move to.'

'Alright' she agreed crossly, 'I never thought of that.' I laughed smugly.
'Do you know mother? I don't know what you'd do without me.'
'Be a lot better off,' she grumbled re-entering the house. I watched her go, a thoughtful expression on my face, then loaded what rubbish was left onto the pram, pushed it to the tip and tipped it over the edge.

On my way back I met a neighbour. A smile crept over her face as she eyed the pram. 'That looks a lot easier to push than my old wheelbarrow. How would you like to take a load of rubbish down to the pit for me tomorrow?' Of course I said yes and took not one load but two, earning myself a shilling.

Word soon got round about me and my dilapidated old perambulator. We were in great demand. That week I earned two pound and sixpence, all of which (according to my mother) had to go in my money box for a rainy day.

All my customers had mentioned, that if there was anything amongst their rubbish that I wanted, I was to help myself. One day to my great delight, I found a saucepan. It was just what my mother wanted, she was always saying she could do with one that size. Saucepans were still very rarely available in the shops. Due, as my mother was often heard to say 'This accursed war.'

I rushed home in great excitement, pulling the pram which bumped along behind me. Giving such a joyous shout as I neared our door. 'Mum ,Mum, look what I found for you, a new saucepan, just what you needed.'

'New saucepan,' came my father's voice, as he came to the door instead of mother and took it from me.

Chuckling he turned it over in his hands, ' This isn't new, it's got a pot mender in the bottom.'
'Yes,' I explained, ' but its new to us and its better than the one mother has got. Her's has got two pot menders in it.'
Next day I had a good haul. I bought home a pair of curtains, which unfortunately didn't fit our windows. Two very rickety chairs took my fancy. I carried them home in triumph. Then, when I sat in one to try it out, a front leg dropped off. I also found a very pretty chamber pot with the handle broken. I told my mother it looked as if it had hardly been used. It was so pretty with those bluebells painted around the side, that I didn't feel I could leave it amongst all the rubbish.

A couple of flower pots, a garden fork with a broken handle for Father, a glass vase with a crack down one side. There was no end to the good things people were throwing out. Good job I didn't hear what my mother told Grandma. 'That child! she takes a load of rubbish to the pit for somebody, then brings half a load back here. I swear I have got more rubbish laying around now, than I ever had before I started turning out.' Well I had begun to think my family a little ungrateful, when I bought home those beautiful treasures for them recently.

The date for our proposed departure rapidly approached. People became more and more troubled and distressed. Those with small farms and business worried constantly about their livelihood. Would they get adequate compensation for their losses and be able to start anew, or was this the end of all they had strived for?

When meeting anyone now, people didn't often say, 'Good morning' or 'Hello how are you?' it was usually, ' Have you found anywhere yet?' The reply more often than not would be, 'No, have you?'

A few days later however, things began to brighten up. A neighbour came rushing home from work early. Eager and excited he ran down the path to our door, banging on it loudly with both fists. 'I think,' he gasped breathlessly, as mother opened the door, 'I think, well I'm almost certain, that I've found somewhere to go,'

'You have?' she exclaimed in delight, knowing instinctively what he meant. So pleased that somebody had found a place to move into, though secretly she wished it was her, so all the worry and uncertainty was over.

'I don't think you understand,' he gasped still breathless. 'What I'm trying to say is, I've found three houses all in a row: one for myself, one for my mother and one for you if you want it. They are rather run down, need a lot done to them, but we can do it gradually, once we move in. Well what do you say?'

Apparently she didn't say anything for quite a while. Mother had been rendered speechless. The relief was tremendous, almost overwhelming. She had recovered however by the time I came home from school. My eyes stood out on stalks as my mother and neighbour, clutching each other tightly, danced madly round the garden. Broad grins on their faces, so pleased and relieved, that at last the end seemed in sight to their constant worry, and the future more secure and settled.

Arrangements were quickly made. At the end of the week my mother and the neighbour's wife would cycle over and view the properties and see what they thought about them. As it was a long way to go it would be a whole day affair. They suggested taking a few sandwiches and drink, and perhaps one or two cleaning utensils to make a start on cleaning the houses. We were all walking on air. Packing began in earnest. In my eagerness about moving house, I didn't seem to mind so much about leaving everything familiar, or my dearly loved relatives behind.

Things didn't quite go according to plan however, for the very next day, we all had a letter to say, there was now no need for us to move, as the Government had now chosen a different, more appropriate location.

Chapter 11 The Evacuees

Anybody that would be involved had been warned. Another batch of evacuees was on its way. Unfortunately as yet, they were not quite sure how many, or if they had found enough suitable homes for them.

A distant cousin of my grandmother, poor old Alice Parkins as she was known, was a spinster who lived in a tiny cottage in the next village. When approached she had grudgingly declared, that if she had to, she would, but it would be under protest mind, take in one little girl and one only. Alice knew nothing whatsoever about little boys, except for the fact, she'd been told they differed from little girls in that, they had a little tail.

On the night in question, Alice was aroused from her slumbers, by loud persistent knocking on her front door. Striking a match to light the candle, she saw the hands on her alarm clock, pointed to half past twelve. Grumbling and muttering about the bad manners of some folk who visited others in the dead of the night, she heaved her reluctant body out of bed, slid her feet into her slippers and tottered down the stairs.

'Who's there?' she demanded. 'Who's there on my doorstep, waking up innocent folks at this unearthly hour of the night?'
'It's me Miss Parkins,' came the answer. 'I came to see you about taking in an evacuee last week, I expect you remember me,'
'I do indeed,' muttered Alice to herself, 'I'd recognise that la-di-da voice anywhere.'
She hurriedly unlocked the door and found to her dismay, not only was the woman herself standing there, but three evacuees as well.

'I really am most terribly sorry to wake you Miss Parkins,' gushed the woman. 'For me to arrive so late and unexpectedly, must have been a shock. The train bringing the evacuees was apparently, unavoidably delayed, due I hear to a very bad air raid. We have done our very best to sort out the children and to deliver them to their new homes, but alas, we have run into difficulties and find we have these three lads left,'

'They are brothers and have no wish to be separated, as you can quite understand. It has got so late now, Miss Parkins, it seems hardly fair to trail these children round anywhere else, so we have decided, the best thing to do is, leave all three with you for the night. I do hope this will not be inconvenient for you. I expect someone will contact you in the morning, to see how you are managing. 'You've got your luggage boys haven't you? Good, then I will say good night and thank you Miss Parkins. Oh and good luck.' Alice was dumbfounded. So far that woman hadn't given her a chance to say a word. Now she stood listening as the woman abruptly departed and the sound of a car that had brought her, died away into the distance.

'How much longer have we got to stand out here?' grumbled the older boy, 'all night? In case you don't know it Misses, we have been on the move since early this morning, we are cold, tired and hungry.'

At his words Alice sped into action. Ushering them inside, she lit the candle and gazed round at her three visitors in horror, still half wondering if she was in the middle of some horrible nightmare. 'You are real aren't you?' she cried in confusion. 'And there are three of you? One of you is taller than me and you've all come to live here. Oh lordy, I was expecting one little one without a tail.'

Her lip quivered, she burst into tears. However was she going to cope with all these boys, when she didn't know anything about boys? The two younger ones, seven and ten years old were upset, understandably so after all their upheaval. They began to cry as well, until Rufus their thirteen year old brother, a big strapping lad with ginger hair and freckles, shouted impatiently. 'My god, pull yourself together do Misses, stop that blubbering! you're upsetting my brothers. If you want something to do, find us something to eat, we are starving.'

Alice disliked being ordered about, especially in her own house, but nevertheless his sharp words did the trick. Alice went into her larder and returned with a new loaf of bread and pot of raspberry jam, the jam ration she allowed herself for the month. Placing it on the table, she watched in horror as the oldest boy sliced up

106

the bread, spread it with the jam from the jar, which had emptied alarmingly and it rapidly vanished down three hungry throats.

At long last Rufus sat back patting his stomach. 'How about some drink Missus? Come on jump to it.' Alice wasn't sure what to make of this cheeky young man and rose slowly to her feet. The boys all looked at her giggling, thinking the situation hilariously funny. Pursing up her lips in disapproval, she lit the primus stove, boiling the kettle to make three cups of cocoa. It took all her remaining milk. Alice also made the mistake of putting the sugar bowl on the table, then watched open mouthed as the boys dug their spoons in. Her sugar ration dwindled rapidly.

Lighting another candle, she stood waiting patiently for them to finish their drinks, then led the way up the narrow stairs to her tiny back bedroom. 'The best thing to do, is push them two small beds together,' she said sharply. 'You will have to make the best of things, I wasn't expecting three of you to come, you know.'

'Of course you weren't.' Rufus put his arm round her, hugging her exuberantly, nearly lifting her off her feet in the process. 'Shall I tell you something?' he said softly. 'You aren't such a bad old biddy after all. To be honest I quite fancy you, I see you've got a double bed in your room, my two brothers can sleep in here and I will sleep with you.'

He grinned wickedly at the expression on her face. 'Don't worry, I'll wait until you're asleep before I join you.'

'What?' snapped Alice, her mouth hanging open in shock, then realising she hadn't put her teeth in, she closed it with a snap. Pushing his arm away abruptly, she stepped back away from him, feeling frightened out of her life as the big, tall, strange boy towered over her.

'You will sleep with your brothers tonight and like it,' she shouted, feeling it was time she let him know who was the boss in this house. 'If there isn't room, one of you will have to get comfortable on the floor. Now no more nonsense.'

Feeling satisfied that she had had the last word and put that boy in his place, she stormed off downstairs, feeling angry at the boy's behaviour. It was a long time later, after giving his words a lot of though! that she dared to venture back upstairs to her room. Even then she peered dubiously round the door, as if half expecting to find that ginger headed rascal, fast asleep between her sheets.

Leaving a nightlight burning on top of her chest of drawers, she laid down on top of the bed, still wearing the old overcoat she used as a dressing gown, also her tattered well-worn slippers. For her protection, should it be needed she tightly clasped her niece's old hockey stick that had been left behind years ago, after a visit.

Time seemed long as she lay awake, well into the early hours, wondering and worrying what might be going to happen. Would that young man who was so full of himself have the audacity to enter her room, force himself on her and rape her? Alice gave a shudder.

Well she had lived nearly seventy years, without being married and certainly didn't intend to be interfered with by some young London whippersnapper. She had it all planned, she knew exactly what she was going to do, if he tried anything. She'd hit him on his tail with the hockey stick, that's what she'd do, that should deter him, stop any tricks he might have up his sleeve.

She tried so hard to keep awake, forcing her eyes to stay open, but against her will they slowly closed. It seemed she had only just dozed off, when a loud hammering on her bedroom door, shot her into instant wakefulness.

'Oh my God no,' she moaned as she raised her head and looked towards the door.
'This is not going to happen.' Gripping the hockey stick tighter, she shouted as loud as she possibly could, 'What do you want boy? Get back to bed immediately.'

There came a short silence, then a voice called, 'No I can't, I need you urgently, do you mind if I come in? Alice's voice was shrill and rather panicky as she answered, 'Yes I do mind, go away at once or I'll scream, I will, I'll scream so loudly I'll be heard over on the other side of the village. And that's no idle threat,' she muttered.

In spite of her warnings, the door opened and there stood Rufus in his birthday suit. Poor Alice who had never, ever seen a naked man before, just didn't know where to look. She was too shocked to scream, falling back on her pillows she waved the hockey stick weakly, with limp hands.

'Please,' he begged earnestly, stepping closer, there came a whimper of fear from Alice and that gave her strength. She sat up and tried to scramble off the other side of the bed. He stopped and stared at her in amazement, ' I say, what do you take that thing to bed with you for, is it because you haven't got a man to keep you warm?'

Alice made no answer, with her feet now firmly on the floor, on the other side of the bed, she stood up and turned to face him, waving the hockey stick menacingly. 'Get back to bed boy. Don't ever enter my bedroom again, without my permission, is that understood?'
'I'm sorry' he sounded quite contrite, 'I only came to fetch you, because my little brother is ill. Usually when he is like this, my mum comes and looks after him but,' he gave a sniff, 'she isn't here is she? My little brother has asthma, he's ever so bad.'

Immediately Alice threw down her hockey stick and dashed into the other room, Asthma was something she knew a little bit about, her own sister had been a sufferer. After that she sat up for the remainder of the night with the boy, who was so bad, any second she thought he was going to die. From then on Alice got on well with her young charges, but was most relieved when, three days later, they were re-homed.

Chapter 12 The Prototype Plane

Another catchy little ditty was doing the rounds, it seemed everyone was singing it,
'Whistle while you work, Mussolini made a shirt, Hitler wore it, Chamberlain tore it, wasn't he a twerp.'

What a shock a school friend Helen and I had, when coming home from school one afternoon. Right out of the blue a plane dived on us. We screamed in fright at spotting ominous black crosses painted on its wings. With one accord, we dropped our bicycles and jumped into the nearby ditch.

The plane zoomed away, screaming to turn in a circle and came swooping back, only just above the tree- tops. We crouched down low in the foul smelling mud, hoping the pilot hadn't seen us, yet we half expected him to machine gun us.

It wasn't pleasant in the ditch, but as Helen said 'At least it was safe.' Swiftly, she suddenly stood up. 'My bike,' she muttered worriedly, reaching out for the handlebars and somehow managing to pull it towards her.

'Hitler's old plane isn't going to have my bike,' she declared, giving a monstrous tug so the bike slid into the ditch right on top of us. I was muddy before, but now sitting on my backside, bicycle atop, I was covered. Not only that, a very damp feeling was soaking through my rear.

After pushing the bike aside, I managed to stand up and was about to scramble out when I spotted a long worm, it hung down from the top of the ditch, its other end swaying about, within an inch of my face. I screamed and screamed and Helen screamed too, although she didn't know what I was screaming for. I had hated worms ever since a boy had put one down my neck. We were still screaming when the rest of our school mates came along and stood roaring with laughter at the sight of two heads poking up from the ditch. When they had had their bit of fun, one grabbed the worm and slung it away. Then and only then did two mud-covered figures emerge from the ditch and what a state we were in.

The others had been lucky, being a bit further back along the road. All they had done was dive off their bicycles on the bank under a large oak tree. In the newspaper next day, it said a German fighter had terrorized school children on their way home from school. It was thought that as no shots were fired, that he was out of ammunition.

What excitement there was, as we had caught out first glimpse of the new fighter. We had heard so much about it recently. It was called a Lightning and was flying round quite low one afternoon, as we came back from school.

This plane was easily identified. It had twin bodies, so differed greatly from other aircraft that flew over. We considered it a novelty. After watching it fly round for a while, we carried on home. I told my mother as soon as I got indoors, that I had at last seen the new plane. Then I hurried upstairs to change.

While I was there, my mother called to say, 'Your friends have just been to the door. The plane you were telling me about has apparently crash landed on a field down near the church. They are going to see it and have started walking. They thought you could soon catch them up.'

This was amazing news. After the excitement of just spotting the plane flying round, we would now have the chance to actually, see it on the ground, but why couldn't my friends have waited a few minutes for me? Never mind, it wouldn't take me long to join them.

Never had I moved so fast, down the stairs and out the door, almost knocking my father over on the path in my enthusiasm. As he reeled back he shouted angrily,
'Hey you, where's the fire?'

I didn't stop. Soon I was racing along in the middle of the lane as fast as my legs would go, determined to catch up with my mates before they reached the plane. Although I was going full pent, it was a long time before I saw any sign of them. Then it was just a glimpse before they vanished round the next corner or bend. It appeared I wasn't the only one running; they were too, running along as if their lives depended on it. At the sound of a bicycle bell from behind, I veered to the side, slowing down and turning my head as a voice said, 'I know where you're off to. You're going to see that aeroplane that came down aren't you?'

'Yes' I replied looking at the grinning face of Will, an older boy. I was surprised when he said,

'Thought I'd go and have a look too. Do you want a lift?'

'A lift.' My face brightened. Of course I wanted a lift that was exactly what I did need. 'Yes please' I gasped. 'I want to catch my friends up, but its hard work. They are miles in front of me.'

Then I gazed at his bike. Where was I going to sit? There was no carrier on the back. As it was a ladies model it had no crossbar either.

'Forgot I'd got my mother's bike.' He muttered sheepishly, 'The only place you can sit is on the handlebars.'

Well, I'd travelled that way before in an emergency and what was this if it wasn't an emergency? I hitched myself up before he changed his mind.

'How am I going to see with you sitting there?' he muttered, ' I can't see through you.'

'Stop grumbling,' I grinned feeling on top of the world. 'It isn't everyone that's got a little gnome sitting on the front of their bike you know. I'll guide you. I'll tell you where to go, a little bit to the left my man,' I put on my talk. 'Now a bit to the right, left a bit, right a bit. We are in the middle of the road, so keep going straight.'

After several wobbles, we eventually made a fast but erratic course and it wasn't very long before I began screeching in delight. 'Hurry up. I can see my friends, Try and go a bit faster. Go on! Pedal up.' In my enthusiasm, my swinging legs moved backwards and forwards as if I was propelling us along.

'Here steady on,' he shouted, 'I can't see. Sit still.' But I couldn't, I laughed and shouted at the top of my voice.

'Here I come gang! Here I come! I'm on the London Express, whooo whooo!'

Just before we reached my pals, who stood staring open mouthed, the bike struck the bank with a mighty jolt and I flew off, right over the ditch to land on my bottom, on the sharp stubble of a freshly cut cornfield.

To the consternation of my friends, who thought I was deranged; I sat giggling in raptures, with one arm outstretched pointing to the Lightning which sat in the far corner of this very field. I found no words to describe it. It looked so beautiful sitting there, like a silver bird, gleaming with the evening sun shining on it.

I finally rose to my feet, tottering off across the field, in the wake of the others who had only stopped for a few seconds to commiserate with me, then laugh as I moaned about how sharp the cornstalks were. They had recently been cut with the binder.

As far as we could see, only one airman stood near the plane. He took no notice as we cautiously approached and stood a short distance away, staring, as children do. A few minutes later we realised he had gone, striding away back over the field, so we crept closer, reaching out with our hands to caress the shiny, smooth surface of the wing, then the tail and the twin fuselages.

'Peculiar looking thing,' commented one boy thoughtfully, reaching out to give the plane a pat.
'Peculiar' I thought, most certainly not. It was awesome and yet, lovely. I had never been this close to an aeroplane before and was relishing every second. Wouldn't it be wonderful if I were a pilot and could climb up into that cockpit, start the engine and fly off into the sunset.

'Hey look at this?' a shout brought me back to reality. 'There's a bullet hole in the engine cowling.' There was a mad dash round to the front of the plane, so we could all have a look. Each and every one of us fingered the little hole, wondering if that was the cause of the plane's downfall.

The airman hadn't come back. He was talking to a group of sightseers, who had been walking over to take a look. With nobody to stop them the boys got more daring. One climbed up onto the wing and went to have a peep in the cockpit, another went to follow and accidentally moved the aileron at the edge of the wing. The next minute his mischievous fingers were moving it up and down. The lad peering in the cockpit was getting excited, 'Hey, do that again. It moves a lever in here. Try the elevator on the tail someone.' Soon four boys were clambering up on the plane, but their luck suddenly ran out. They were spotted and someone shouted. The airman was seen running back over the field, but I had spotted something much more serious. My mother and great auntie were heading towards us. How thankful I was, that I was still on the ground, not yet having managed to climb up.

My mother eyed me suspiciously, but said nothing. When they had looked at the aeroplane, walked all round it and admired it, spoken to several more people who had now arrived, they left to go home and I had to go with them. As we left, more airmen were arriving and two huge flat back lorries were trying to manoeuvre through the field gateway.' In the morning the plane had gone. Yet every time I passed that field for weeks afterwards, my eyes were drawn to that far corner, where that beautiful Lightning had sat there in the sun.

Chapter 13 American Planes

These days and nights too, the sky above roared and throbbed with the sounds of aircraft engines. There were fighters there too, but mainly it was huge bombers such as Liberators and Flying Fortresses. They were two of the biggest culprits. Especially if they were preparing to go on a raid. Although several miles distant from the nearest airfield, on a clear, still day, the noise of aircraft engines revving up on the ground, prior to take off could be clearly heard.

My family with perhaps a neighbour or two or friend, would stand on our garden path listening intently. 'Be another one up in a moment,' my mother would declare and sure enough, another plane would heave itself up into the sky, loaded to the very limit with bombs, fuel and ammunition, to join others already circling overhead.

We would wonder where they were off to. My mother would say, 'Where ever it is, some poor innocent souls will be killed. People like us who didn't want this war anymore that we did.'
'But they are Jerries!' us children would shout, 'The more of them that's killed the better.'
What hate we had for the Germans. As far as we were concerned they were responsible for all our troubles. Bloody old Germans; damned old Jerries ought to be shot the lot of them, at least that was our childish verdict.

As the bombers began flying over heading for the coast, the noise was deafening. Sounding as if the whole sky was full of swarms of giant insects. We would try to count them but there were so many, our scores never tallied, always more went out than returned.

On their outward journey, still flying low, not yet having gained sufficient height to get into formation, we would wave like mad, shouting at the tops of our voices, 'Good luck mate. Give old Jerry a pasting. Make Hitler run like the devil! Give him a piece of shrapnel up his bum! Keep your wits about you. Don't let old Jerry get on your tail. Safe journey. Mind you don't get shot down.'

Of course they couldn't hear us. Just as well sometimes, the things that were shouted. I doubt they even noticed us down here on the ground, having far bigger things to contend with. The crew were probably in their appointed positions, preparing for the journey ahead. The pilot at his controls, straining his utmost to persuade the gigantic aircraft to gain more height.

'I say just look at him?' My mother was pointing to a particularly low plane. 'It's got such a load on board, you can almost hear it groaning with the weight. It's all he can do to get along. That pilot needs guts to do what he's doing. Getting that lot up off the ground alone is a major operation, without flying it across the sea to enemy territory. One little error, just one little slip, that's all it needs to create a terrible disaster.'

What thoughts were in the minds of the crew we wondered, as we watched them fly out over the North Sea. Could it be their loved ones? Were they wondering if they would ever return? Would this be their last trip? Might they be killed or captured, sent to a prisoner of war camp for the duration of the war. Or destined to be blown to pieces by a direct hit, so going from here to eternity, heading straight to hell.

A school friend laughed when he heard us. Wittering on as he called it. 'The crews concentration will be on the job in hand,' he said 'It's complicated flying an aircraft, there is the navigating, finding the target and dropping the bombs, looking out for danger from enemy planes, who will be doing their utmost to shoot him down. Besides that, trying to evade the flak flung up from the ground.'

Occasionally, after the planes had all gone over, we would hear the sound of one returning, 'What's brought him back?' we'd ask each other. We would watch with hawk like eyes, listening in case we could detect any irregularity in the tone of the engines. 'Sounds alright,' we'd mutter. 'Perhaps his guns have seized up, can't go over to Germany or wherever he's going if they don't work. That's asking for trouble.'

'Might not be that, might be something wrong with his bombsights,' said another, 'or one of the crew might have been taken ill'. There was no end to the excuses we made for him and no means of satisfying our curiosity. Sometimes we would hear that plane circling around for hours to use up fuel, before being allowed to land.

Some Liberators were so low when they flew over, we could clearly see the pictures painted on the sides of their noses. We got so we recognised individual planes. 'There goes Donald Duck, Pegasus and the Rattle Snake,' They always laughed when they mentioned that one, because they knew I hated snakes.

The word snake made me shudder; being one of those people who imagined every stick laying in the grass was a snake. Not that I'd ever seen one. Only pictures and that was bad enough. Recently though, I had been extra vigilant, for rumour had it the American airmen at the base, had brought over a real, live, young rattlesnake as a mascot.

Somehow it had escaped; I'd overheard the adults talking about it. My grandfather had said 'Rattle snakes come from a warmer climate than ours, when the winter comes it will probably die of cold, if they haven't killed or captured it by then.'

This was no consolation to me, I was on tenterhooks the whole time, expecting any second when I was out, to hear a gigantic hiss, followed by a spine chilling rattle and a diamond shaped head shoot out, from the bank or hedge to bite me.

Father was the first to notice the plane with a young lady painted on its nose She was dressed only in a bra and panties. He called her Tulip. The rest of the family referred to her as the near naked lady. The plane was around for weeks, and then suddenly she disappeared. Naturally there was much speculation as to her fate. Had she been shot down, or just moved to another airfield? We never found out.

My favourite Liberator was the one with a Red Indian Chief's head on its nose. I always looked out for him when the planes went over, being very distinctive with his head-dress of yellow feathers and face adorned with war paint. Unfortunately after a few weeks he too disappeared, much to my regret.

117

One afternoon when the bombers were due back, a little Walrus seaplane came over heading for the coast. 'The bombers won't be long now,' predicted my mother looking skywards, 'I hope nobody is in trouble, I always worry and think there might be, when I see that little plane go over. I don't know what his job is, but wonder if he's ready to pick up survivors if a plane can't make it home and has to ditch in the sea.'

We didn't have long to wait, for soon the sky was filled with the roar of returning aircraft. With a sudden squeal of brakes, a school friend arrived on his bike. 'Are you coming for a ride?' he yelled coming to an abrupt halt. Before I could answer he pointed excitedly upwards. 'Gosh look up there. He's got an engine out of action. The prop is feathered, look!'

We watched, spellbound as my mother drew our attention to another one. This had bullet holes sprayed all along the fuselage and one particular very big hole. For a second everyone was quiet then somebody cleared their throats and spoke, their voices barely above a whisper. 'My God look at him?'

'Be lucky if they haven't got casualties on board,' came a mutter. 'I don't think they will keep him circling around for long, when he gets home. I bet he goes straight away.' That poor old plane unfortunately, wasn't the only one to suffer damage. Wherever those bombers had been, as my friend said,
'They hadn't half had a pasting.' This was the worst we had ever seen them come home.

Presently a Liberator flew into view, with a chunk missing from its tail. It looked strange and peculiar, as if a giant had stepped by and taken a bite. However we were grateful to see, that at the moment it didn't appear to be affecting the manoeuvrability of the plane.

One came in now with damaged wing and feathered prop, the wing looking blackened as if the engine had been on fire, the flames reaching back over the whole wing. But worse was to follow. We all felt some degree of fear as one flew towards us, making the most awful noise. We could tell immediately there was something dreadfully wrong with it. One engine was already out of action, another obviously causing great concern. Roaring and grinding, sounding very rough indeed.

Out of the blue now, came an ear-shattering explosion from the plane. I nearly jumped out of my skin in fright, feeling tense and ready to run. 'It's alright,' grinned my school chum taking it all in his stride. 'It's the engine, I think it backfired.' We watched anxiously as another shattering explosion rent the air. The engine cut out. 'Oh dear God,' whispered my mother, 'Help those poor lads up there.'

'Keep going, please keep going plane.' We put heart and soul into willing it to go on. Slowly it began to pull away from us and we all uttered a huge sigh of relief. We could still hear the engine banging occasionally, the engine cutting out as the pilot battled on. We watched until he was out of sight, expecting any moment to see the plane go down and hear the explosion as he crashed.

We expressed our concern to a neighbour, who had just joined us but he shrugged it off. 'Don't worry about him, he's probably nearly out of fuel, but he's got two other engines so he'll get home.'. The rest of us weren't so sure we all had our fingers crossed.

There came a bit of a lull now. The main force seemed to have gone over. Now it was time for the stragglers. 'One coming now,' shouted my friend with glee. Then he gasped. 'My god look! look! look! He's in trouble he is.' The Flying Fortress was coming in low, only just clearing the treetops. One engine feathered and another leaving an ominous trail of thick oily black smoke. It was obviously losing height rapidly.

Then all at once, down she went out of control. One second she was there and the next, she had gone. Almost immediately came the sound of an explosion and plumes of thick black smoke filled the air.

For a second nobody spoke or moved, we were too stunned. Gazing at the spot from where the plane had vanished, disbelief in our eyes. Finally my chum game me a nudge, 'Shut your mouth, its open wide enough to sink a battleship in.' He grinned,

119

'come on, what are we waiting for? Get your bike out of the shed and hurry up. That plane isn't far away, we'll ride round and try and find it.'

It was one mad dash to fetch my bike. As we set off my mother shouted, 'Be careful, and don't get in anyone's way.' 'Alright,' I shouted back and pedalled furiously after my friend. The other returning aircraft were forgotten as we headed up the path and onto the road.

We had no idea where to go. We just headed in the direction as best we could, towards the tell tale smoke. Round this corner, round that, over the main road and through the tiny country lanes, even weighting up the possibility of taking a short cut over a ploughed field.

It was further than I had anticipated I thought, as I puffed along behind my leader, who seemed determined at all costs, to be the first one on the scene. Snatches of song floated back to me as he sang, 'We're coming in on a wing and a prayer. We're coming in on a wing and a prayer. Though there's one motor gone we can still carry on, we're coming in on a wing and a prayer.'

'We are getting close,' he shouted back, 'I can see the flames as well as smoke coming up. Come on, pedal up.' As we rounded the corner of the lane there it was, over on the far side of the field. We threw our bikes down on the bank and scrambled through a hole in the hedge so we could see better.

Although we could hardly have taken ten minutes to arrive, we were not the first on the scene, already some twelve or so people were hurrying in various stages over the field towards the plane, so we ran to catch up to the nearest ones and tagged on behind.

As we drew nearer, we could see there was more than one fire. A great big one and several smaller ones. Fire engines from the base were already there. Padded figures with hoses were standing right in amongst the blazing wreckages. 'Oh look at them, they'll be burnt up,' I gasped voicing my thoughts out loud. My friend, braver than I, had left me to go closer, so an old man took pity on me.

'They'll be alright me gal, don't you fret. They are well protected. What they are trying to do is get close to the body of the plane, to make sure there is nobody left inside it. Some of the crew got out, do you see. Jumped with their parachutes on, just before the plane went down.'

'Yes it's the pilot that's the worry,' another old chap joined us. 'He didn't stand much of a chance. Neither did them others really. They were much too low when they jumped. I don't know how many survived, but there is a dead one laying over near the gate as I came in, they had covered him up with his parachute.'

'If that pilot is still inside, he's Sunday joint by now, poor young fellow. Some mother's beloved son no doubt; some pretty girls sweetheart. Let's hope he was killed when the plane crashed so he didn't suffer.'

All at once, there was considerable activity amongst the flames. Muffled shouts were heard, but not distinguishable. All eyes were turned to the scene. 'I reckon they have found him,' commented my new friend in an awed sort of voice.
'Aye, I reckon you could be right,' agreed the other old chap, pulling his cap from his head in a token of respect.

To our amazement, strange things were now happening. The fire crew were running from the fire, one or two of them gesturing to the people watching as they did so. Reluctantly the group nearest the fire began to move back, then after more shouting they took to their heels and ran on past us.

A women yelled 'Come on. Shift yourselves, unless you want to be blown up. They say there might be a bomb in the wreckage.'
'What did she say?' I asked the old man I was standing with. But our other friend made no comment; he had taken to his heels and was heading for the far hedge as fast as his old legs would go.

The woman shouted again, 'Get away you stupid old man. Get the child away. There's a bomb in the wreckage.'
'A bomb,' he muttered. 'Hear that gal, run, and run for you life.'
My legs belted across that muddy field, but young as I was and fast, I couldn't catch the old man. As I told my mother later, he

must have been nearly seventy, yet he galloped across that field like a two year old.

Mud and pieces of straw accumulated on the bottom of my shoes, impeding my progress. Suddenly I lost my footing and slipped over. Too frightened to get up and run again, I just laid there, folding my arms behind my head and waited for the inevitable. Would there be a big bang? Would it blow pieces of the blazing aeroplane about? Would any land near me, or more importantly, on me? My poor heart thudded in fear.

Then there came a series of small bangs- ammunition, not a bomb. Laughing and joking the people surged back past me to their original position near the plane. I struggled to a sitting position and looked around. The firemen were back at work as if nothing had happened. I was the only person down this end of the field.

Rising on unsteady legs I tottered over to join the others, closer than I had been before, congratulating myself on being so brave and mastering my fears. But it was short lived. There came a sudden crack, crack, crack, crack from the fire as more ammunition exploded. The firemen began to run, as did the front group of people.

Unfortunately as one big teenager turned, he bumped straight into me knocking me flying. Such was the force that I fell over backwards and him with me. I lay flat on my back all the breath knocked out of my body and felt rather than saw the boy get up. The sound of his running stirred me. I looked round to see I was the only person near the flaming, roaring inferno.

Rising shakily to my feet I fled in sheer terror. Halfway across the field my shoe flew off, landing a little way in front of me. With so much impetus behind me, I ran on past it before I could stop, I didn't want to stop, but thought it better to face the hazards of the aeroplane rather than my mother if I went home without it.

Before I'd got across the field, the watchers were on their way back. More and more people were arriving all the time. There was quite a crowd now. More ammunition popped off, but this time nobody moved back. Somehow I felt I'd had enough. I was exhausted. My school chum I had arrived with seemed happy with a group of other lads. There was no way that I was going to trudge across that field to tell him, I had decided to go home.

I waited a while, just in case they ran back, then taking a last long look at that blazing inferno and all the people now standing round it, as close as they dared go, I slipped back through the hole in the hedge, picked up my bike and began to pedal home. Thinking no one would ever know the terrible fright I had endured. I still shook with the realization of knowing that a bomb may have gone off at any second, whilst I was laying on the ground so close to the plane.

The nearer I got to home the better I began to feel. I was pleased and relieved when it finally came into view. Whilst running from the plane, a thought had crossed my mind: if a bomb went off, would I ever see my home and family again? I dumped my bicycle against the wall and hurried indoors, impatient to tell my mother all about it.

Instead of my mother, I was amazed to see Jean my elder sister sitting there, looking pale and shaken. She was fourteen now and had recently left school and had a job where she lived in. Today was her half day, she had been on her way to spend it at home when she heard the plane coming in low. Somehow knowing by the sound of it, it was coming down , she managed to fling herself from her bicycle onto the nearby bank, numb with fear.

For several seconds she had lain transfixed in fright, eyes pressed tightly shut, afraid of what she might see when she opened them. Thick black smoke drifted over. The roar of the flames was deafening. Jean said she knew she had to move and her eyes flickered open, suddenly lifting her head she stared straight through the hedge in astonishment. Staring back at her, equally bewildered, was a member of the crew who had landed by parachute.

The following day, I had a grand time at school, bragging all about my sister and her miraculous escape from the plane. I explained how it had come down, forcing her off her bike and nearly killing her. Everyone was so interested, but as I dashed home on my bike at the end of the school day I had far more important things on my mind.

I managed to cadge the crust off a new loaf and spread it with dripping, then I was off again. Having just cycled over three miles from school, huffing and puffing with the urgency to get home, I was now pedalling away again, to accomplish what I considered to be a very important mission.

Chapter 14 The Trophy.

I chewed and laughed to myself as I pedalled furiously through the lanes, on the same course as yesterday, wondering which was going the fastest, my mouth or my feet. Then a piece of crust slid uncomfortably down the wrong way. I had a coughing fit, so had to slow down.

I knew exactly where I was heading and didn't have to rely on a thick pall of black smoke to guide me. Arriving at my destination, I leaned the bike against the bank and scrambled through the same gap in the hedge as yesterday. But as I straightened and glanced around the field, expecting to see the remains of the crashed aircraft, I had a shock. There was nothing there.

Nothing at all, except two cock pheasants strutting proudly, one behind the other, across the far corner. I stared and stared, I knew enough about crashed aircraft in wartime, to know they weren't left in fields for long. In case, as the older boys had told me repeatedly, a German spy came poking around, hoping to fathom out secrets from the plane and report back to Germany. But this time yesterday, the plane had been an inferno. Surely it would have needed time to cool down before being moved?

Bewildered and strangely angry, tears of disappointment welled up inside me. I began to think I'd had a wasted journey. Surely all my hustle and bustle hadn't all been in vain? My hopes, my plans, my lovely, lovely plans. I gulped hard to keep tears at bay.

The latest craze at school was to make rings and brooches out of Perspex, the stuff aeroplane cockpit covers were made from. Unfortunately, this precious material could only be obtained from a crashed plane. The boys at school had become quite adept at their new hobby, explaining to me at some lengths, how easy it was done, using a red hot poker or very long nail. When finished they were a work of art, even having a flower or other patterns fashioned on the front. I had felt so envious when shown these rings, even more envious when some of the boys presented their rings to their girlfriends. The unfortunate thing was, I had no boyfriend, so therefore no ring.

I did so want one of those rings. When I saw a boy showing his around, I offered to buy it, but as I only had tuppence, the boy refused. He said after all the hard work he had put into making it, he wanted a fiver at least. Well five pounds in these days was an absolute fortune. Anyway, in exchange for my tuppence he let me fit the ring on. Just when I was thinking how well it suited my fingers, he snatched it back and slipped it into his pocket.

I gave a resigned sigh and bit my lip in frustration. It looked as if the only way I was going to have a ring, was find some Perspex and make my own. The aeroplane crashing yesterday had seemed like the answer to my dreams.

The aeroplane was gone and it felt so scary here, deserted and lonely with no houses nearby. So different from yesterday when other people were present. I hadn't realised it would be so frightening on my own.

After thinking it over, I decided I had two choices: either go back home and forget about all my plans, or put my fears behind me and go and take a look. Just how badly did I want that Perspex? If I could find any.

The lure of a ring was too strong, I found myself running, seconds later, across the field as fast as I could go, heading towards the far corner where the plane had been. Only when halfway across did I have second thoughts. Nobody seemed to mind these days, if you went on their land to look at a freshly made bomb crater or crashed aeroplane, but when the crater was filled in or the aeroplane moved as in this case, then legally I had no right to be here, I was trespassing.

Feeling vulnerable out here in the open, I made for the hedge and ran alongside that. I knew when I'd arrived because of the huge blackened patches of earth. Immediately my eyes scanned the ground searching, for the precious material I needed so badly.

The ground was littered with tiny minute fragments of metal, but nothing that I yearned to find. I ambled up and down and round and round, then just when I was on the point of giving up, over near the hedge I found a piece. Only a small piece but large enough to make a ring, not content with this, I kept on searching and soon came across two more pieces, slightly larger than the first. I was over the moon with joy. Now I shall be able to have a ring I thought; two or three if I wanted. I'll make the other girls at school envious. Perhaps they will even think that at long last I'd got a boyfriend.

I wanted to prolong my search, but the evening was drawing in. I dare not delay any longer. So I ran back across the field, grabbed my bike and pedalled home through the darkening lanes.

Though brimming over with excitement, I told nobody about my find and sat back to await my opportunity, a time when the family was out and I had the house to myself. That time came the following Sunday afternoon. Father went off to play cards with his mates and my mother and younger sister to visit grandma.

I made the excuse to stay behind by saying I had arranged to play with one of my friends. My excuse was accepted and nobody was in the least suspicious or thought I had an ulterior motive.

Standing at the door I watched them all out of sight, then gleefully recovered my precious piece of Perspex that I'd hidden. The fire in the cooking range had been dampened down with potato peelings, underneath there was just a faint glow. I rammed the poker into the very heart of the fire, grabbed the newspaper from the table and vigorously flapped it up and down in front of the grate.

For a minute or two nothing happened, then a small flame appeared. Only the instant I stopped flapping, it disappeared, so I had to keep on, flap, flap, flap. Eventually the newspaper tore and it was today's! Goodness what was my father going to say when he saw it? He would be most displeased. Also my arms were beginning to ache with all this flapping. Things weren't going quite according to plan.

Impatiently I withdrew the poker, it was getting hot I was pleased to see, but not yet hot enough. I pushed it back in with a sigh of impatience and ran to the door, to make sure nobody was coming home earlier than anticipated.

Again I withdrew the poker and this time the tip was nicely red, I couldn't help shouting and leaping into the air with exuberance. 'Hey ho, the operation is about to commence.' Holding my smallest piece of Perspex between finger and thumb, I gently lowered the tip of the poker. There was a kind of sizzling noise, in an instant, the room was filled with a thick acrid white smoke.

This astounded me, where had that come from, I looked round but my eyes were streaming I couldn't even see in which direction the door was. Evil fumes caught my throat, making me cough and choke until I could hardly breath. The Perspex had long since slipped from my nerveless fingers and lay together with the hot poker on the hearth rug.

Suddenly I became aware the door had opened. An angry voice was shouting, 'What the blazes is going on in here?' It was my father. Grabbing me by the shoulders he almost threw me outside into the fresh air. After a bad coughing fit himself, he held his handkerchief, wetted in the rain water butt, over his nose and mouth, went back inside to open the window wide.

Smoke and fumes were pouring out, but they didn't seem to abate, so venturing inside once more, he dragged out the rag hearth rug, which was now well alight. As he stamped out the flames, he saw the poker and remainder of my Perspex laying there. It was a dead give away.

When we had both recovered, I had to explain what I had been doing, I got a good talking too. Never, ever again, must I experiment with hot pokers and pieces of crashed aircraft, for the next time if something happened, there might not be anyone to rescue me.

It was only by chance he said, that he'd come home for something he had forgotten. Had he come home ten minutes later, I could have been dead. I learned afterwards, the boys at school made a bonfire, to heat their poker in and tied something round their faces, before making a start. But like I told them when they called me an idiot, nobody had told me.

Chapter 15 The War Effort.

How quiet the classroom was, apart from the 'click, click, click,' of knitting needles and the occasional whisper to our classmates, everyone was industriously knitting. Our teacher, a member of the Women's Voluntary Service had arrived that morning with a bundle of white wool.

'This is your chance to do a bit towards the war effort' she had said. 'Vests are needed for homeless people, those bombed out of their houses, who have lost everything and have nowhere to go.'

Several children such as me, who didn't knit very well, were persuaded to have a go. It was quite simple we were told. Just a matter of casting on a certain number of stitches. Each row was the same; knit six, purl six, all the way across. When we came to the neck, we had to cast off some stitches, knit the two shoulder straps, cast on more stitches again and knit the back, nothing could be easier.

Against my better judgement, I was given two ounces of wool and a pair of knitting needles, then like my friends around me, I made a start. It wasn't too difficult, quite fun really, sitting beside the others and all knitting furiously. Occasionally measuring mine against somebody else's to see who had done the most.

We were allowed to take our knitting home with us. My mother seemed pleased that evening as I sat indoors knitting, 'doing something useful for a change,' she had muttered, instead of playing outside.'

I knitted as fast as I possibly could, hoping to outdo everyone else at school and finish my vest first. The only drawback was, my hands got so hot and sweaty and I had forgotten to wash them before making a start. Consequently, my knitting was no longer white but a dirty grey colour, in places black.

Feeling ashamed to have let it get that colour, I pulled it all out, discarded the wool and made a fresh start. Halfway up the back, the same thing happened. Out it came once more. After the third time my mother got so cross, 'You do realise,' she said 'that if you pull it out anymore you won't have enough wool to finish it.' Oh the relief when I finally did!

My mother stitched it together for me and crocheted round the neck. Grandma brought a piece of tape to thread through the holes my mother had left. But in spite of all the care, the finished product was still too grubby to take back to school. In the end my mother washed it.

When I did finally pluck up the courage to take it back, the teacher looked at it thoughtfully, but made no comment. 'Would you like to knit another one?' she asked. 'Or perhaps consider knitting a pullover, for the soldiers or sailors, like some of your friends are doing?' my answer was a horrified 'No.'

My mother had seemed just a little bit envious when I had been doing my knitting, she knew it was no use her offering to help me because she was absolutely no good at it, but strangely she could crochet beautifully.

One afternoon, right out of the blue she had a visitor. A woman dressed in naval uniform. She didn't beat about the bush, once she had established who my mother was and came straight to the point. 'I hear you can crochet?'

'Yes, yes,' came my mother's startled reply, 'but of what interest is that to you?'

'A great deal. You're the person I'm looking for,' said the woman with a smile. 'If I might come inside for a few minutes, my dear, I'll explain.'

She produced a large mitten from her bag, explaining that it had been cut from an old coat. The palm and the back of the hand had been crocheted in fine string and stitched on afterwards. 'Could you do that?' asked the woman, looking anxiously for her reply.

'I most certainly could,' my mother answered in a flash. 'There is nothing complicated about that.' The woman was thrilled and said she had only two other people in the whole county that could do it and string mittens were urgently needed for the lads on Mine Sweepers who used chains to explode mines. At long last, my mother was able to do her bit for the war effort.

She also began disappearing every Saturday morning I thought she had found herself a little job, until her friend let the cat out of the bad. She came round one morning and said, 'Isn't your mother back from her lesson yet?'

'Lesson' I said 'What lesson?' and so of course the secret was out. My mother was learning to fire a rifle.

'Why does she want to do that?' I enquired indignantly.

'Because,' I was told, 'if those blasted Germans ever invade the country we are going to need people like your mother to defend us.'

I thought it over for a second or two, then I smiled, I felt so proud. I could just visualize my mother with a rifle and me at her side with my 'bayonet' ready to have a go at the German troops. Perhaps, I thought I'd better pull my bayonet out of the hedge and sharpen the point up a bit more, for I was determined to jab a German with it and make him run, before the end of the war.

Chapter 16 Butterfly Bombs.

Every child in the school was packed into one classroom, waiting in anticipation for we knew not what. Extra chairs had been brought in to ensure everyone had a seat, although we were a bit crushed up together.

We were beginning to feel restless, when finally a knock came on the door. 'Sir,' as we called our headmaster, went to open it and came back with two members of the ARP dressed in uniform. One carried a briefcase. The other had a short cane tucked under his arm.

After being introduced to the other two teachers, one laid aside his briefcase and helped to set up the blackboard, the other came to the front of the class. Smiling at us he said ' Good afternoon children.'
'Good afternoon Sir' we shouted giving our best performance. Obviously he wasn't used to quite such an ovation, for his hands flew up to cover his ears.

With the blackboard now up, the briefcase was opened, various papers and posters taken out and pinned to the board. 'Now children,' said the man who had spoken to us. 'We are going to mention our enemy I expect you all know who that is.'
'Yes sir' we screeched at the tops of our voices. We liked this sort of thing, 'Adolf Hitler, the Germans, old Jerry.' The words came thick and fast.
'He's, Himmler, Goebals,' the boys were in their glory until Sir stepped forward, with a no- nonsense look on his face. Then the shouting died away.
'Let's just say the German's,' said the man. 'Now, not content with dropping bombs on our houses, hospitals, factories, streets and shops, they are now targeting our youngsters, yes young people like you. They are dropping fiendish, devilish contraptions to injure and maim.'

He pointed to a boy sitting near the front, then to the poster on the blackboard. 'You lad have you ever seen one of these before?'
'No Sir,' answered the boy shaking his head, 'No Sir, I've never seen anything like it.'

The stick pointed to another boy, 'You son. If you found one of these, what would you do with it?'

'Pick it up most probably and take it home I guess,' came the answer.

'And then?' prompted the man,

'Guess I'd put it in the shed and try to take it to pieces some time.'

'That's exactly what I thought, that's what the Germans want you to do, but you wouldn't get that far Do you know why? Does anyone know?'

There came another silence. 'Right let's have a further look at the poster. It says Spitterbombe, anti personnel butterfly bomb. Yes, it's a bomb now being dropped by the enemy. Anyone finding one of these, picking it up and trying to take it to pieces, will unfortunately suffer severe consequences.'

'It will explode, not necessarily to kill you, but to severely injure, maim or disfigure you. For instance, if you were holding this bomb in your hands when it exploded, it would blow your hands off.'

'You,' he pointed to a girl in the back row. 'Look at the picture carefully. Tell me why you think it's called a butterfly bomb?'

'Because its pretty,' she answered after a moments hesitation. 'It's attractive.'

'You,' the cane pointed to another girl, 'If you found this laying in the grass, what would you do?'

'Pick it up I suppose,' she answered, 'to see what it was.'

'Precisely. That's what the Germans intend you to do,' he nodded. 'Now lets look at our bomb in a little more detail.' He turned the poster over to a large diagram and with his cane pointed out the various parts. He was a good talker and had an enthralled audience. He ended up by saying, 'if you come across one of these butterfly bombs, while you are out walking or playing, there are three very important things to remember.'

'The first is, do not touch. The second is keep your distance from it. The third is to report it to the first adult you meet, be it man, woman, police man, doctor, parson, member of the ARP or Home guard. Any of these people will report it to the right quarters. Then it will be dealt with.'

'One more thing before I go and leave you to your lessons. If there are two of you, when you find one of these, it might be a good idea for one to go for help, the other to stay within distance of the bomb, so you can warn other children or adults that come along to keep away from it. That way you will save lives. That's all I have to say to you children. Good day to you.'

I dashed home after school, eager to tell my mother everything the man had said. She listened attentively then said, 'Well you've got no excuse child. You have been warned, so be sensible and heed the man's warning. If you find anything like it while you are out, for goodness sake don't touch it.'

Next morning being Saturday, I went off in search of my mates. They were very evasive and it took me a while to track them down. Eventually hearing voices from a field gateway, I investigated and found them all there, also surprisingly, school chums from the other end of the village, plus three older boys who had recently left school and whom I didn't know.

One looked round and saw me as I timidly approached, 'Come on girl,' he shouted. 'You can join us if you like. We are going butterfly bomb hunting.' Goose pimples sprang up all over me. I couldn't resist a shudder. Butterfly bomb hunting! Why that was the last thing I wanted to do.

Although I was scared, I felt I couldn't refuse to go, as everyone else appeared eager to set off. If I backed out they would probably call me a cowardly custard, or yellow belly or worse and exclude me from anything else that they planned another time.

Sticks were now being broken from the nearby hedge and handed round. Soon everyone had been supplied with one and we trotted off behind our three investigators. Round the sides of the fields and meadows they led us, searching the hedgerows, ditches and undergrowth. We came to a wood and went all around the edges of it, poking and prodding, peering up into the trees, in case a bomb had come down and got caught up in the branches.
We moved further and further afield, finding ourselves at last in unknown territory. We had seemingly progressed through the outskirts of the next village and were about five miles away from

home. I think we would have been going yet, if a farmer hadn't spotted us and told us in no uncertain manner to, 'Bloody well clear off home and don't come back.'

When we returned footsore and weary, we had found exactly nothing, for which I was extremely relieved. I had the feeling that if we had found one of those butterfly bombs, the bigger boys would have hit it with their sticks to explode it, or thrown stones at it, but luckily all ended well.

Chapter 17 Doodlebug

Our neighbour asked if we had heard the strange sounding aeroplane that had come over during the early hours of the morning. It made such a dreadful, unusual sort of noise. Just hearing it, she said, frightened her to death. It sounded as if it had something badly wrong with it and was about to crash.

This gave rise to a lot of speculation. What could it have been? Fortunately we had all been asleep at the time, so hadn't heard it. There had been no rumour of a new type of plane flying round.

However at school that day, we had another visit from the two ARP members. Being in a hurry as they had other schools to visit, they got straight to the point. 'Good morning children, we are here to inform you of Hitler's latest weapon. Some of you may already have heard or read about it in the newspapers. The German's call it Wergeltungsaffe, but don't twist your tongues round that, its known to us by several much simpler names, VI, Flying bomb, Buzz bomb or the most common name of all, Doodlebug.'

'For several weeks now, these little machines have been made and launched from France. They fly over the Channel and make their way inland to London and other big towns. Eventually of course, the engine stops, it dives to earth and explode, causing endless damage and often, loss of life.'

'Due to the heavy bombing of their launching sites, these flying bombs are now being carried by planes such as the Heinkel and Junkers 88's. Released out here over the North Sea, just off the coast, all the Doodlebug has to do is run the gauntlet of the guns and make its way inland. The VI or Doodlebug is only a small aircraft, on average about twenty feet long, with a wingspan of sixteen feet and made almost entirely of plywood and sheet steel. Here,' he pointed to a diagram now pinned onto the blackboard, 'is the explosive warhead which is fastened to the fuel tank, seen here in the body of the plane, close to the wings.'

'It has no pilot, so the course it is to travel on is pre-set. It can reach a height of 2.500 feet and travel at about four hundred miles an hour.' He pointed out various other things on the diagram, such as compressed air bottles, the automatic pilot, the height and range controls and the mechanism that operated rudder and elevator. Then he pointed to what he said was one of the most vital parts.

'The long pipe mounted on the end of the fuselage, is where the jet engine is situated. From out of this end comes a long flaming exhaust, which gives the impression that the plane is on fire. It makes a horrendous noise as it chugs along, spluttering and roaring across the sky.'

He went on telling us more and more about this little machine, I was so fascinated, I wanted him to go on talking about it, but of course he eventually came to a stop. After putting away their papers, diagrams and pamphlets, the two men left. That was all great fun I thought, for not only had I enjoyed it, it had got us out of doing lessons for half the morning, what a pity it couldn't have been for half a day.

We sat indoors that evening, my sister Eliza and I, my mother having gone to visit our neighbour next door. Suddenly she came running back. 'Quick, come outside and look. Something peculiar is coming. It's making an awful noise, sounds as if it can hardly get along.'

We dashed out immediately, peering up at the darkening sky, towards the direction of the coast and then we saw it. 'Good Heavens,' gasped my mother, 'It's on fire. Look you can see the flames. Those poor boys up there must be terrified. Much as I feel for them, I hope the plane keep going, at least until it's gone over us.'

'That isn't a plane,' I suddenly shouted, a note of panic in my voice. 'It's one of those things they were telling us about at school today. It's a Doodlebug.' Three pairs of eyes watched as if mesmerized. Nearer and nearer it came. Now we could just make out the shape of the Doodlebug, in front of the flaming tail.

'Dear God,' muttered my mother, 'keep that thing going. Let it come down in some field where it won't do any harm.' Now almost overhead, the roar of the Doodlebug was deafening, it seemed to paralyse us, leaving us rooted to the spot. All I could think of was, another few minutes and we would be safe.

Hopefully it would go over and disappear into the distance.

Then with no warning, the engine cut out. The flaming tail vanished, one minute it was roaring away and the next, an ominous silence filled the air. An awful eerie feeling came over us, I thought at first my heart had stopped too. I was so terrified until I realised I was holding my breath. 'Indoors quick!' Roared my mother, a touch of desperation in her voice.

She didn't have to repeat herself. She just gave us a shove. We flew through the doorway and landed in a heap under the table. 'We'll be alright,' I muttered, though who I was trying to convince I wasn't sure. Certainly not myself, for I laid there in a cold sweat, shaking from head to toe and trying to remember what we had been told at school about this thing.

When the engine stops, the Doodlebug glides slightly to the left, or was it the right? In my panic I couldn't remember. The silence was ominous, I'm sure we all imagined that the Doodlebug was gliding down towards us.

Then came the explosion, the floor seemed to tilt and heave beneath us. The whole house shook. Windows rattled and pheasants in the nearby wood screamed out in fright. My mother struggled up, taking her weight off my legs. 'My God,' she cried, 'I wonder where that landed, I hope to God nobody has been hurt.'

The siren now went, sending out it's mournful, moaning, wailing warning of danger. We heard it clearly through the half open door, that my mother in her panic to get us inside, had omitted to close.

'Bit late now,' she grumbled, 'letting that thing through without warning us it was coming.' The guns along the coast were firing, a few minutes later another Doodlebug was heard approaching and that terrible fear began all over again. This was on the same course as the last one, coming straight towards the house. There was dead silence under the table. We hardly dared to breath as we strained our ears to listen, waiting for the engine to stop, at the same time hoping and praying it would keep going.

It did. My mother scrambled out to have a look and we followed, just in time to see that flaming tail disappearing into the distance. There came a terrific barrage of gunfire, followed by another stuttering roar. 'Are you scared?' asked Eliza.
'No of course not,' was my reply. 'I'm not scared. I'm absolutely petrified!'

The next few minutes was like bedlam, with the distant roar of aircraft, guns firing, in the midst of it all, I suddenly thought of our neighbour, sitting all alone next door. I clutched my mother's sleeve but her attention was on the approaching Doodlebug.

'I expect poor Annie is scared all by herself,' I shouted. This time it brought the desired results. She flew round,
'Goodness gracious me, how could I have forgotten her. 'Quick, before that thing arrives over us.'

We took off like a herd of stampeding elephants, racing round to our neighbour's door. I arrived first with my sister a close second. My mother had to lean over us to reach the door and open it. There was no standing on ceremony those days. In our struggle to get inside we grazed our knees on the rough coconut matting.

'I hoped you wouldn't be long.' beamed our neighbour. 'Have them things finished coming over yet? I thought if I couldn't hear them I wouldn't be frightened, but I still am,' Despite the blood-curling roar just passing overhead, we burst out laughing, for she sat in her chair with a great pad of cotton wool over each ear, tied in position by a thick crepe bandage, that went round her ears, over the top of her head and was somehow tied under her chin. Fortunately that Doodlebug was the last to come over that evening, but we stayed for half an hour, until the siren sounded the All Clear.

The Doodlebugs continued to come over, sometimes just the odd one, sometimes several one after the other. Early mornings or evenings were the worse times. We would hear the German planes going backwards and forwards along the coast, awaiting the opportunity to release their Doodlebug, so they could be on their way home.

Not once did we ever hear them coming, without suffering that terrible spine-chilling fear. Was the engine going to cut out, or was it going to keep going. They were very tense moments.

Then came the worst night of all. I awoke suddenly during the early hours, to hear gunfire, aeroplanes flying over and worse, I could hear the stuttering roar of a Doodlebug. Quickly climbing out of bed, I made my way over to the window, where my mother stood listening.

'Wake you did it? She asked, 'I don't wonder at it. There's a tremendous amount of activity going on out there. The German planes are flying up and down like mad and our planes have gone out there to try and shoot them down, before they have a chance to launch their Doodlebugs. There have been more guns than usual too, as if some more have been drafted in. At least three Doodlebugs have already gone over and by the sound of things another one is imminent.'

'Just listen to those guns, they are firing like demons,' her voice quickly changed to one of horror. 'My God, I believe they have hit it, but its still going. What a dreadful noise it's making.' We dashed back from the window and were about to wriggle under one of the beds for safety, when there came a tremendous orange flash. So bright it burst right through the blackout curtains at the window, momentarily illuminating the entire room. Then it was gone. Almost at once came the most monstrous explosion.

A loud, rumbling sound followed which seemed to fill the whole sky. It was as if the heavens were spilt apart, so fierce and violent was the aftermath. My mother eventually found her voice, 'My God,' she muttered, 'they hit it, the thing blew up.'

She crept back to the window, carefully lifting a corner of the blackout curtain and peering out cautiously, as if trying to ascertain where the Doodlebug had come down. Meanwhile the Bofor guns started up their boom, boom, boom again, as if aware of their victory, determined for their luck to be resumed with another Doodlebug. Mother said the sky was full of tracer and looked like a firework display, but I couldn't be tempted to go and watch.

Half an hour later things quietened down and I returned to bed. Not so my mother, she went downstairs, opened the door and looked out. Mother was very, very brave on these occasions. Had she heard voices she would have called to see whom it was and if every thing was all right. Any signs of fire close by she would have got out her bicycle and rode off into the night, to see if there was anything she could do to help. She wasn't the only one, most people were like that those days, everyone willing to help should the need arise.

Next morning the postman told grandma, the Doodlebug had been hit by a shell and eventually blew up, the wreckage coming down in a farmyard about a mile away. It was agreed that after we had come back from school and had had our tea, we would all go and take a look.

I was ready first and standing outside impatiently waiting. When grandma and great auntie arrived we set off. Eliza, the only one of us without a bicycle, sat on the back of mine. We led the way. Behind came great auntie, then mother, both riding their tall upright machines with a basket on the front of the handlebars. Bringing up the rear was grandma, tail end Charlie we called her.

Our little cavalcade took up all the road as we pedalled single file along the narrow lane, no wider than a cart track. Soon we came to the farmyard and leaned our bicycles against the hedge. Seeing there was nobody about we walked inside to take a look. I was disappointed when I saw nothing, I think like the rest of us I was expecting to find almost a whole Doodlebug sitting there.

But apart from piles of old rusted farm machinery and implements dotted around, over grown and partially covered in rubbish, we saw nothing. 'What a mess everywhere,' sighed great auntie as she wandered along in front,' and just look at that old stovepipe laying over there?'

We looked and laughed. Auntie's stovepipe was the cylinder that had been mounted on the back of the Doodlebug, housing the jet engine which of course was no longer there. But one end was blackened and cocked uppermost as if that was the end where the flaming exhaust had shot out as the fiendish machine had chugged towards us. Apart from auntie's 'Stovepipe' we saw nothing else but a few pieces of what looked like scrap metal laying around.

It had felt good to have a laugh, if it was only over a simple things like 'Auntie's stovepipe' which as you can guess that particular piece of Doodlebug was so named forever. My young sister confused a few of her friends one day, when a Doodlebug came over as they were walking to school. 'It's a Doodlebug,' screamed one, 'Hurry up, let's hide.' They dashed to the hedge and hid behind it. Then my sister feeling brave peeped out.
'It's a nearly gone.' she said. 'All I can see is auntie's stovepipe with the flames coming out the end of it.'

After a few weeks the Doodlebugs got fewer and fewer then ceased coming altogether. There was talk now of a new weapon, supposedly to be worse than the Doodlebug. It was called the VII. I listened to all the talk about it with dread. What, I thought, could possibly be worse than the Dreaded Doodlebug.

The VII or rocket was a different thing altogether, with a long cylindrical body of about forty feet in length. The diameter around its widest part was said to be five feet.

It had stabilising fins at the back and a long nose, which tapered to a point and contained the warhead. It was said to take only four minutes from launching to reach its target. Although they were said to come over us we didn't actually see any. They were far too high and fast. Although we did see vapour trails in the sky that the boys told me had been left by rockets.

EPILOGUE

Now my story is coming to a close. Soon I would be fourteen and have to leave school and make my way in the world. The war wasn't over by any means, fighting continuing to go on in many countries and our men folk were still overseas in the thick of it.

But thankfully we could now go to bed and look forward to an uninterrupted night's sleep, without the fear of German planes roaring over, loaded with bombs and landmines or other devilish contraptions and the dreaded Doodlebugs with auntie's stovepipe on the back. Also the VII's had ceased to come.

Much to our regret, sweets were still on ration, as was food. Nothing had altered in that respect and probably wouldn't for a long time to come. I had grown up, in spite of the majority of my childhood years being spent during this accursed war.

No longer was I a small child who believed everything I was told. I now knew you didn't chase a German with a bayonet to make him run, you stabbed him, well to put it bluntly, in the guts so he couldn't run. The older boys had told me. My biggest regret of the war was that I hadn't met a German to use my bayonet on. For several years I had been so hopeful of this happening.

On Tuesday 8th May 1945 Churchill told the nation, ' Yesterday at 2.41 a.m. the representative of the German High Command ... signed the act of unconditional surrender of all German land, sea ,and air force in Europe...Hostilities will end officially at one minute after midnight tonight ...but in the interests of saving lives the "Cease Fire" began yesterday to be sounded all along the front ....The German war is therefore at an end.....Long live the cause of freedom. God save the King!'

Now for us this dreadful war was more or less over. How grateful I was that I and my family had survived this stressful time and we now had a chance to live a normal life. Many poor people hadn't. We were the lucky ones, and father and I now had a better understanding since the day he saved my life.

Coronnol

An End of the Universe Story

by
Philip Alan Tyler

Published by NQGE Books